DATE DUE

SOLDIER, SAGE, SAINT

SOLDIER
SAGE
SAINT

ROBERT C. NEVILLE

New York
FORDHAM UNIVERSITY PRESS
1978

Printed in the United States of America

Dedicated to
LEONORA HORTON EGAN
and
JAMES MARION NEVILLE

Contents

Preface

THIS BOOK IS A PHILOSOPHIC STUDY of some aspects of spiritual development, construing the field of spiritual development in a broad way without essential connection with organized religion. My sense for the contours of the field has been influenced significantly by comparisons between several of the world's great spiritual traditions, and I have tried to be faithful to experiences in those traditions. Readers whose interest in spiritual development comes from the excitement of non-Western traditions will find this book congenial in this regard.

This is a *philosophic* study, however, not a manual for becoming liberated or a scholarly monograph on the exact meaning of spiritual development in some tradition or other. The book puts forward a philosophical theory of spiritual development, paying attention to personal, social, and metaphysical concerns, and analyzing three central images of spiritual "heroism." It is aimed at students of philosophy in the broadest compass of that class, and requires some effort at philosophic thinking. Although some of its basic systematic strategies may be limited in interest mainly to professional theologians and philosophers, the book's point of view, its arguments, and the experiences on which it is based are accessible to anyone willing to study philosophically. I believe that people with mature interests in spiritual development are natural philosophers and that the challenge of hard ideas is more worthwhile than the pap of popular conclusions.

The central contribution attempted here is a way of understanding the quest for spiritual liberation or perfection in terms of the models of the spiritual soldier, the sage, and the saint. At times it seems that the argument aims to promote spiritual liberation itself, not merely to understand it. This surely is true. From a philosopher's point of view, our society desperately needs viable forms of spiritual development, and lamentably is lacking them. One of the reasons for the lack is that concepts of spiritual development often evoke an hostility which derives from philosophic poverty. If this essay contributes to better philosophic understanding, then it is promoting spiritual liberation, and the hortatory passages should be taken as such.

This purpose comes from a philosophic love of useful wisdom, and should not be confused with a lesson from a spiritual master to a world in need of salvation. Although I have a philosophic love of reason as the art of living, I possess no particular accomplishments regarding spiritual development. The spiritual experience on which much of the argument is based is not my own in any vivid way but rather the funded experience of the spiritual traditions, open to all for investigation and surprisingly accessible to empathetic inquirers. What a philosopher shares most closely with all spiritual seekers is the task of becoming responsible. Everyone has an obligation to learn to be responsible in every domain of life; this is the sense in which everyone must be philosophical to some degree. The spiritual areas of life are perhaps the most important in which to attain responsibility, and the most difficult. Those of us who aspire not only to being philosophical but to being philosophers find that responsibility in spiritual matters to be a joint concern with those who think of themselves as spiritual seekers.

Why listen to a philosopher about spiritual development who himself is not a spiritual master? I have often wondered about that myself. The answer is, for the same reason that philosophers are interesting, if they are, when they talk about art without being artists, politics without holding office, or science without performing experiments. Philosophic thinking attempts to provide a way of seeing things in context and in connection with other things which is not available from the standpoint of the enterprise under investigation. Of course, if there is a spiritual master who is also a philosopher, he should have the priority of attention. But spiritual mastery seems to be a rather open field these days.

Any author who thinks systematically, as I do, feels insecure in saying anything without saying everything. In books, this means an obsessive urge to footnote oneself. Clearly, my highest spiritual attainment to date is to have abandoned this narcissism in the present book, except for Chapter 5 where it is directly relevant. The pain of this discipline is only bearable, however, because I am now going to say in general how my other books provide detailed arguments for what is only asserted in this one.

God the Creator presents a very long and detailed argument for the conception in its title, which is also employed below. Its third and fourth chapters explore the senses in which God can be said to be Being or Non-being, on which the question of theism and atheism hangs. Its fifth through eighth chapters deal with the bearing of experience on theological and philosophical knowledge. The ninth relates the conception of God to religion. The tenth analyzes what religion's central problem is, and the eleventh through thirteenth explore this through internal and external aspects of religious life. These are important supplementations of the discussion of spiritual development if it is borne in mind that religious matters and spiritual ones are not identical, as distinguished in Chapter 1 below.

The Cosmology of Freedom provides a complex analysis of the various dimensions of personal and social freedom summarized in Chapter 1 below. It was originally conceived as a study of personal, social, and spiritual freedom, of which the theme of the present book was to have been a third part. But the kind of analysis and argument appropriate for spiritual freedom is different from the others and stands better alone. The "cosmology" in the title refers to a categorial interpretation of what it is to be a person in a physical and social world; this categorial scheme is summarized briefly in Chapter 2 below, and consequences are drawn from it at various places in the book. The third chapter of *The Cosmology of Freedom* contains a discussion of value which attempts to justify many of the claims made in the present book about how anything with a structure has a value which can be appreciated absolutely.

Soldier, Sage, Saint is systematically related to the earlier two books. *God the Creator* argued that everything determinate is created directly by God. How can human life then be conceived to be free from God, or at least free enough to be responsible? Is not the creation theory the very worst form of Calvinistic predestinarianism? *The Cosmology of Freedom* presented a picture of the human world showing how certain determinate things are related to other determinate things in various ways, making up the dimensions of personal and social freedom. Personal and social freedom consist in having something like those determinate connections and, where required, indeterminate relations; in principle God could create a world determinate and indeterminate in just the right ways to be free. Whatever is empirically possible, God *could* create. But the problem of mankind's freedom over against God is most acute in spiritual matters where the creator's presence may be seen as special intervention. Hence, *Soldier, Sage, Saint.* Chapter 5 makes this explicit.

Many people have contributed essential ingredients to this work. My interest and concern for the problems of spiritual development were first raised by my parents and by Raymond Sturgis and Andrew Smither. The colleagues and students at Yale and Fordham Universities who were acknowledged in previous books are also due thanks for inspirations in the present one. Those at the State University of New York College at Purchase have contributed ideas, criticisms, and dialogue directly to this book: Marcia Cavell Aufhauser, Steve Denison, Boris Kiriako, and George Wolf have been particularly helpful, and many others will find their marks here; Jay Schulkin provided the most substantive criticism by insisting that spiritual enjoyment without spiritual responsibility is fraudulent. Thomas Berry introduced me to the spiritual literature of India and China, demonstrated its importance, and guided me through it. The feeling I have for many of the main concepts of spirituality has come through the study of T'ai Chi Ch'uan, for which I am limitlessly indebted to Sophia Delza. For the preparation of the manuscript I owe thanks to Angela Pecararo, Isabel Murray, and Donna Simmons. The book is dedicated to my paternal grandfather and to my wife's paternal grandmother.

State University of New York
  Stony Brook

SOLDIER, SAGE, SAINT

1

Models of Spiritual Perfection

THE SOLDIER, THE SAGE, AND THE SAINT are ancient models of spiritual perfection. The ideal soldier is the model of psychic integrity. The sage is the model of enlightenment. And the saint is the model of perfection of the heart. Different cultures have explicated these models in many overlapping ways, often inconsistent with the neat usage suggested here. This book is not an historical study, however, and, indeed, will develop the models according to philosophical constructs to be discussed shortly. But a brief characterization of the models at the beginning will indicate that there is much historical plausibility to the distinctions involved.

According to the ancient model, a soldier in the heroic mold must have psychic integrity to such a high degree as to be able wholly to devote himself or herself to life-threatening tasks. The attention, intensity, and presence-in-action required of the warrior are taken to be the norms for anyone who must have psychic integrity in the face of life-and-death issues. Reflection on psychic integrity, in fact, suggests that human existence itself bears the problem of being "truly alive." After telling the Hebrew people, for instance, that their integrity consists in adherence to the covenant with God, Moses said, "I call heaven and earth to witness against you this day, that I have set before you life and death, blessing and curse; therefore choose life, that you and your descendants may live" (Dt 30:19). The associations of this remark with military metaphors, however unconscious in the minds of the Deuteronomic editors, are illustrated by the fact that immediately following this speech Moses exhorted his audience toward their impending campaign to win territory in Canaan, and introduced Joshua as their warrior-leader. Besides Joshua, traditional examples of the spiritual soldier include Arjuna, the warrior to whom Krishna's yoga in the Bhagavad-gita was addressed, the samurai whose spiritual home is Zen Buddhism, the warriors in Castaneda's rendition of the teachings of Don Juan, the chivalrous knights of medieval Christendom and Islam, the disciplined Jesuits following the Father General, and the Methodist circuit riders with Wesley's *Discipline* laced to the Bible in their saddlebags. Common to all these renditions of the model is the conviction that the soldier must abandon any thought of self which might interfere with action-for-its-own-sake. The ideal soldier is a hero of discipline who has attained psychic integrity, with all the physical accompaniments of that.

The sage is a model for spiritual enlightenment, which has been described in many inconsistent ways. Even among closely related sects of Buddhism, enlightenment has meant both consciousness of transcendent realities and consciousness that there are no transcendent realities. But common to the principal discussions of sagacity is a distinction of enlightenment from secular knowledge and wisdom. Secularly learned and wise persons are commonly thought to know the relative importance of things and the ways those things are connected; because of this they may act with due respect to the important things in life. Sages, by contrast, know how to interpret the affairs of life with respect to their ultimate meaning, however "ultimate meaning" be interpreted. Whereas the attainment of wisdom comes from long experience, the attainment of a certain level of sagacity might come as *an* experience, such as that of the Zen Buddhist who is suddenly enlightened to the emptiness of all things. Sages, furthermore, might be factually ignorant and practically unwise; Chuang-tzu, the Taoist, virtually advocated this. On the other hand, sagacity might be connected with certain esoteric kinds of knowledge as in Upanishadic Brahmanism, Gnosticism, or Christian mysticism.

Though related, the model of the saint should be distinguished from those of the soldier and the sage. Beyond both discipline and enlightenment is the perfection of the impulses of the heart. Psychic integrity can keep those impulses in check, and enlightenment plus wisdom can tell what they ought to be; but altering them so as to have only good impulses is another kind of spiritual perfection.

> Confucius said, "At fifteen my mind was set on learning. At thirty my character had been formed. At forty I had no more perplexities. At fifty I knew the Mandate of Heaven. At sixty I was at ease with whatever I heard. At seventy I could follow my heart's desire without transgressing moral principles."[1]

Although all the main cultural traditions have articulated this model, Christianity has emphasized it most, recognizing its call to perfection. From St. Paul to Sigmund Freud, techniques have been espoused for bringing the supposedly involuntary impulses under responsible control. In a sense, sainthood is an even higher triumph of psychic integrity than the soldier's discipline, bringing the very urgings of the heart within psychic control. In another sense, it transforms the problem of psychic integrity from discipline and control into the remaking of individual nature.

The models of the soldier, sage, and saint will be examined in detail in the following chapters. I shall argue that the models expose critical areas of human experience which merit careful cultivation according to the models construed as ideals. But before that it is necessary to clarify what is meant by a model.

II

The phrase "spiritual model" can be taken to refer either to an ideal individual or to an ideal type. I mean the latter in this study. This is an important distinction because, historically, individuals have been put forward as ideal models to be emulated; Christ, Confucius, Lao-tzu, Krishna—all have been "inspirations." But in this study individuals will be taken to express some aspect or other of the model or ideal type. My purpose is to explicate what it is to be a soldier, sage, or saint, and individual heroes will be cited only as examples of these models.

Whether referring to individual or type, however, the word "model" connotes both structured character and value or normative worth. The models of soldier, sage, and saint are represented as somehow good, ideal, as human perfections, perhaps as even obligatory. In what does the normative character of the models consist? That is an extremely complicated question to whose answer every part of this book is intended to contribute.

Some of the complexities of the question of the normative character of the models are explained in the following consideration. According to Eric A. Havelock's argument in *Preface to Plato*, the works of Homer constituted a kind of cultural "encyclopedia" for the Greeks of the archaic period down to the time of Plato when literacy finally became widespread. Since learning and memory were oral during that period, not literate, the "encyclopedia" had a poetic and dramatic form which aided memorization; furthermore, the response of those hearing the Homeric epics was to replicate insofar as possible the emotions and actions being expressed. This entailed an extremely uncritical and immediate response to the literature, a response against which Plato violently reacted and as an alternative to which he invented procedures of abstract, critical, objectifying thought. Achilles, for instance, was the individual model for courage; in times needy of heroic courage, people looked to Achilles both for inspiration and for information about what to do. Plato, however, insisted that Achilles be perceived as an instance of a type, a form, and, by means of that frame of reference, introduced a cognitive distance between Achilles and his imitators which allowed for critical evaluation of the model: to Plato, Achilles seemed like a spoiled adolescent!

Now, insofar as Krishna, Buddha, and Jesus, for instance, are regarded as *individual* models of spiritual perfection, they may inspire people and evoke devotion and imitation. But once the question arises whether they are *really* and *truly* ideal, whether they deserve to be norms for life, they must be viewed as instances of types: perhaps unique instances, but instances nonetheless. The question of the validity of ideals then switches to the worthiness of the type models. Since the time of Plato in the West, the evaluation of norms has focused directly on universal or type norms, and only indirectly on individuals as instances of norms. As the history of Western philosophy has shown, this is not an entirely satisfactory arrangement. Skepticism regarding the ability to justify universal or type norms may be as great today as Plato's skepticism regarding the validity of Homeric individual-model norms. Nevertheless, even if norms cannot be justified (which I believe is a false supposition), the consideration of types at least allows claims to normative validity to be criticized.

One of the responsibilities of intellectual life in the modern world is that it maintain a stance which allows for critical self-reflection. For better or worse, innocence is now irresponsible. Therefore, the choice to construe "spiritual model" as referring to an ideal type rather than to an ideal individual is not entirely arbitrary but stems from the obligation to consider the model critically. Individual models—for instance, Krishna, Buddha, or Jesus—cannot be examined critically unless we consider them as instances of types. A more direct critical procedure is to consider the types: in our case, the soldier, the sage, and the saint.

But exactly how can the types be examined in critical fashion? Plato's procedure in his dialogues frequently was to consider one by one the various aspects of experience to which some norm (for instance, justice, courage, or piety) is alleged to be relevant, exploring the interpretations and interconnections of them all, finally both defining and justifying the norm as a way of harmonizing all those experiential components. Sometimes, of course, no definition could be found; but somehow the participants in the dialogue had come to a better understanding of the area to which the norm was supposed to be relevant.

In a loose sense, that is what will be attempted here with respect to the models of the soldier, the sage, and the saint. By tracing out the ideal types of those models, we shall consider various dimensions of psychic integrity, of various phenomena of enlightenment, and of what it means to transform and perfect the desires of one's heart. One of the intended connotations of the word "model" is that the models exhibit certain structures according to which the subject functions and is composed; models of soldier, sage, and saint exhibit certain structures of will, reason, and heart, respectively. It should be possible to describe and make apparent certain aspects of spiritual perfection involved in those models, and to indicate their desirability. This in no way would constitute a deduction of the normative validity of these ideals from higher principles. Nor will it be possible through this method to justify the perfection of oneself according to any of the models as a moral obligation, a categorical imperative, without the added premises that people have the imperative always to do that which is most worthwhile, and that perfection of oneself is most worthwhile. At best, the analysis can describe recognizable dimensions of experience having to do with psychic integrity, enlightenment, and perfection of desires, showing how the developments of the spiritual models are ways of fulfilling or perfecting these dimensions. In a negative sense, however, it will become apparent that limitations on spiritual development are limitations on the ability to be responsible.

A final ambiguity in the notion of "ideal type" needs to be mentioned here. That phrase in its common sense associations means that the type itself is good, ideal. But in its sociological usage it means a pure type or essence, without accidental features. In this usage there is no suggestion that the type is a good one; hence, there can be ideal types of the hoodlum, the embezzler, the psychopath. Now, insofar as this distinction holds, it is clearly the second, sociological, usage which is intended here. Critical reflection requires that the types of the soldier, sage, and saint be described without smuggling in assumptions as to the worth of being a soldier, sage, or saint. In principle it may turn out that the dimensions of experience revealed in the models are undesirable.

But even in the sociological usage, there is a certain value involved in a type: namely, the cognitive value of grouping certain features together under the concept of the type. The ideal type of the hoodlum is a good *concept* because it groups together certain features of the lives of some people in some societies, in a cognitively useful way. Similarly, the types of the soldier, sage, and saint are cognitively valuable if they sort out and group together relevant features of psychic integrity, enlightenment, and perfection of the heart. A special difficulty of interpretation arises here. If a certain type has to do with human potentialities, and if it can be used as descriptive of one's own potentialities, there is a deceptive temptation to believe that the type is not only a good way to *conceive* of oneself but also a good way to *be*. If a person *could* be a saint, would it not be *good* for him or her to be a saint? Perhaps; but not merely because of the potentiality. That a person could be a hoodlum does not justify taking that potentiality as an ideal, even though some philosophers—Sartre, for instance—sometimes suggest that authenticity might require this. Rather, if the potentiality for saintliness involves a worthy ideal, it is because of the qualities of saintliness. As types, the models of the soldier, sage, and saint can be justified as normative only by showing that they are good ways of integrating elements of experience which themselves are worth integrating.[2]

III

As mentioned above, the models of soldier, sage, and saint are a combination of historical generalizations of spiritual types with a philosophical construct regarding those aspects of life to which the models might be applicable. The philosophical construct is responsible for the demarcations of the models. I shall not attempt here to develop the construct in a fully responsible philosophic sense, attending to the philosophic positions and issues of the day. The construct is needed only for heuristic purposes, to provide a blueprint for drawing out the historically important features of the three models. The philosophical target here is those dimensions of experience illuminated by the models, not the justification of the construct according to which the models are elucidated.

Therefore the discussion which follows is based on a construct drawn from Plato, his division of the soul into three parts: the spirited part (θυμός), the rational part (λόγος), and the appetitive part (ἐπιθυμητικός). Plato's construct itself rests upon distinctions which deeply impregnate Western culture, and it has in turn been extraordinarily influential. Subsequent discussion of the three models will prove Plato's construct to be helpful for understanding non-Western spiritual traditions too, which will enhance its plausibility as a heuristic device.

In the *Republic* Plato first developed the character of the appetitive part of the soul, under the rhetorical assumption in Books II to IV that some people can be *only* appetitive. Appetite has to do with desires, with feeling needs, and with the activity motivated by those needs for their fulfillment. Subjectively considered, the appetites are desires for attractive things, urges which are stimulated to greater fervor by more attractive objects. Objectively considered, the appetites are causal processes by which ideals, or desired ends, are made ingredient in the world. In the *Phaedrus* and the *Symposium* Plato analyzed the character of appetites. Of course, the appetites conflict and are often aimed at low kinds of ends. The function of reason is both to propose more comprehensive goals which sort out consistent appetites and to propose goals with greater fulfillment. The content of life, however, is simply the pursuit of appetites, eros. All human action is erotic in the broad sense, the expression of appetite. The development of virtue in the appetitive part of the soul is to have the higher appetites dominate life and the lower appetites kept in their places. *Reason* distinguishes between the higher and the lower, and the *spirited part* of the soul enforces reason's judgment. But it is the character of one's appetitive make-up, however ordered by wisdom and discipline, which constitutes the content and intrinsic value of one's life.

The spirited part of the soul, said Plato, is a kind of aggressiveness or anger which can be turned against either the appetites or reason. By itself spirit is uncouth. Its education consists in being disciplined so as to be brave and singleminded in addressing obstacles, and gentle and harmonious when dealing with the weak and when resting in itself. The means of its education is "imitation," in physical combat and the arts (*Republic*, Bk III, 410B–412A). According to Plato, the cultural models for spirit should be censored because the imitative spirit by itself blindly takes on the character of its mold. When the spirit is disciplined well, it provides integrity to the soul by causing the rational part to perform the tasks of deliberation and judgment and the appetitive part to pursue the rationally appointed ends. Thus whether one has integrity depends on the education of one's spirit. If one lacks an education, one's anger is directed inconstantly and erratically.

The rational part of the soul has as its main task ruling through discerning judgment. It is concerned with all knowledge, both knowledge of the elements over which rule must be made (which Plato called the realm of becoming) and knowledge of the norms for judgment themselves (the realm of being). The central portion of the *Republic* (Bks V–VI) is devoted to explicating an ideal education for the rational part of the soul. Interestingly enough, in Plato's view, the rational part of the soul would naturally prefer to contemplate its own truths, and must be forced by spirit to engage in its ruling function. Reason and spirit together have as their purpose the perfection of appetite.

In the models presented in the following chapters, the soldier is the archetype for the development of the spirited part of the soul, the sage for the rational part, and the saint for the appetites. In the *Republic* Plato was concerned with the basis of authority, and the rational part of the soul (and predominantly rational people) came out on top, with appetites making the original demands and the spirit providing the integrative instrumentality. Our concern for spiritual models does not share the *Republic*'s priorities. Plato's constructs of the three parts of soul are extraordinarily suggestive and will be used to control the overall outlines of the discussions of the soldier, sage, and saint. I shall develop those constructs, however, with an eye to the internal unfolding of the issues under discussion rather than to Plato's own intentions.

In this section I have tried to provide a somewhat abstract introduction to the main concepts and philosophical strategy of the pages which follow. However preliminary and provisional, this introduction provides a necessary orientation for yet a different kind of introduction. "Spiritual development" is the subject matter to which the models of soldier, sage, and saint are relevant; "spiritual perfection" and "spiritual liberation" are close synonyms to be used where the stress warrants. Just what is spiritual development? Spiritual matters have generally been associated with religion, and religion is a controversial cultural phenomenon. To introduce spiritual development as a contemporary problem it is therefore necessary to discuss both its connection with religion and the state of religion and "spirituality" at the present time. But before that it is necessary to make certain philosophical comments on the nature of spiritual development, and on the way in which it relates to other kinds of personal and social endeavors. The next two sections provide these introductions.

A PHILOSOPHIC DEMARCATION OF SPIRITUAL DEVELOPMENT

I

The word "spiritual" has been used in a great many ways, most of them far too broad to be useful. It has been associated with things religious, for in-instance; but I shall argue in the next section that this is at best an imperfect association. It has been used to mean anything having vitality or life, and Hegel used its German equivalent to refer to the most concrete and inclusive of realities; these uses too are so broad as to obscure important distinctions between the spiritual and the non-spiritual but humanly important dimensions of life. "Spiritual" has also been used as a pejorative label by physicalists or materialists to decry prima facie elements of experience to which they want to deny any kind of ultimate reality. Though I admit that there is always an arbitrary element in stipulating meanings of common words diversely used, I shall use "spiritual" in this book in a way which derives from a theoretical philosophic distinction and yet which makes intimate connection with the literature of "spirituality" from which the models of the soldier, sage, and saint may be drawn.

The most obvious way to see the connection between the spiritual dimension of life and other dimensions is to reflect upon the fact that spiritual development, or the search for spiritual perfection, has often been represented as a kind of freedom, a liberation from spiritual bondage: without psychic integrity one is not one's own master, without enlightenment one is in bondage to illusions, without perfection of the heart one is in bondage to one's own partial passions. Like any kind of freedom, spiritual liberation is an ideal attained under certain circumstances, in varying degrees. But it is unlike other kinds of freedom in many respects, and can be distinguished from personal freedom in its several dimensions and from social freedom.

Personal freedom involves at least the following components. To be free is not to be in chains, and there is no end to the task of discovering and casting off the gross and subtle chains which bind us. But what good is it to be unimpeded if, for reasons internal to ourselves, we cannot act? To be free is, more, to be able to act on the basis of our intentions, organizing ourselves with a clear and powerful will. Yet the intentions themselves may be free or bound, depending on whether we individually choose or blindly inherit them. Freedom, therefore, is also the ability to choose between genuine alternatives, choosing in such a way that the characters which we have as voluntary agents are those which we bestow upon ourselves; no environment or antecedent conditions could make us particular voluntary agents. But we are still in bondage if our options are preformed and we must pick among the world's entrees. A greater freedom yet is found in the creativity of inventing new perspectives and possibilities, in practical skill and judgment in criticizing alternatives, and in cumulative responsibility for actions in an environment which we ourselves have helped to form. All these are dimensions of personal freedom adding up to *autonomy*. Is not autonomy—acting according to the self's own law—the very heart of human dignity as Kant defined it?

However central to human dignity, *personal* dimensions of freedom can be snares and delusions, as any political revolutionary would point out. People can be unaware of the social frustrations which make personal freedom a mirage. The beginning of the *social* dimensions of freedom occurs when a society explicitly prizes and devotes some of its resources to guaranteeing opportunities for unimpeded action or development; personal freedom requires a guarantee in socially recognized rights. The opportunities which any particular society recognizes as rights, moreover, depend on historical fortunes; what one society recognizes, another may neglect. Except in monolithic societies, there will be various systematic discordances between the freedoms enshrined in social rights and the opportunities prized by individuals. A more profound dimension of social freedom, then, is the ideal of a pluralistic society; where people are different, only a pluralistic society can be a free one. Even in a pluralistic society, however, we must find our own ways into appropriate social forms with a style of social life true both to our personal and cultural idiosyncracies and to the political character of the pluralistic society itself; attaining an integral social life is yet another dimension of freedom. Of course, a society offering rights, cultural diversity, and integral social styles must be governed. The society is free at an even deeper level when its form of social organization, its politics, accords with and fulfills the other dimensions; in recent years this has been called "participatory democracy."

Freedom on its personal side seems to be the perfection of *autonomy*; on the social side it is the perfection of *participation*. But even with both kinds of freedom, one still senses that the living waters of freedom have not been captured. Not that the personal and social dimensions of freedom are unimportant or can be skipped over! But there is a certain flatness to the kind of freedom realized in those personal and social ideals. Of course, in the understanding of some people, that is all there is: perhaps most people are aware of only a few of even those dimensions. But for other people the personal and social dimensions do not get to the essence of the subject.

The sense that freedom is more profound than its personal and social dimensions can be elucidated through an understanding of the relations involved in those dimensions. On the one hand, in the pursuit of autonomy people construct themselves (to some degree) by relating to the environment and to the components of their own nature in various ways. On the other hand, a society pursuing participation seeks to enhance individuals' connections with their social environment so that they will be able to participate with greater thoroughness and relativity. In both cases the problem is to deal with relations between *things in the world*. In a theoretical sense, the structure of those dimensions of freedom is to be understood and explained in terms of a cosmology, a "vision of things making up the world." The differences between those freedoms and their opposites are to be understood as differences in cosmology.[3]

What individuals make of their personal and social freedoms on the most profound level depends on the way in which they relate to their own being as such. Of course, the *identity* of people's being, *what* they are, is understood cosmologically, and it includes the people's relations with the world and with their own components. But however broad and inclusive a person's identity might be, the way in which the person relates to that identity *absolutely* is not another cosmological matter. Although there are many ways of formulating this point (perhaps none acceptable to all people), the problem is an ontological one: Why is there this identity (or this world) at all? The most profound level of freedom is reached when a person sees the need to come to terms with his or her own existence, not *what* he or she is but *that* he or she is. "Spiritual" will be used to refer to those aspects of life particularly involved in one's relating to oneself absolutely.

II

The word "absolute" means "by itself" or "non-relative." Any finite thing, with a determinate character, is relative in one respect and absolute in another. It is relative in the respect that its character is defined in relation to its surrounding and internal conditions. A thing is absolute in the respect that it simply is itself; although *what* it is is a cosmological function of its relations, its *being* what it is is its absolute ontological character.

One of the chief purposes of this book is to elucidate this distinction, and it will take the whole book to do so; but a preliminary feeling for it can be indicated here. Buddhists distinguish between living with an attachment to things and living without attachment. The former is relative; the latter, absolute. In some of the earliest Buddhist writings attachment was construed as wanting to hold on to objects for the sake of their contributions to one's ego. But in later writings attachment came to mean living with "intentionality," relating to things as objects of intention in mind, heart, will, or action. Intentionality supposes a distinction of object from intender. Non-attachment, in those later writings, meant recognizing that intentional acts are also things in themselves and can be experienced as such. Enlightenment, in this view, is experiencing the things which one previously had experienced with a new appreciation of their immediate being; that appreciation comes as a shock. Part of the spiritual quest for a Buddhist is for the experience of things as absolute.

In Western thought, absoluteness has been ascribed mainly to God, since only God can be said to exist by himself or non-relatively. The structure of the problem of God in the West is different from that of Nirvāṇa or Suchness in Buddhism. Some thinkers—Thomists, for instance—have argued that God must be conceived to be absolute in exclusion of the world, since a real relation to any finite thing would sully God's perfection. Other thinkers—Whitehead, for instance—have pointed out that this conceives God to be so distant from human experience as to be spiritually and religiously irrelevant; God should be conceived, alternately, as a definite entity within the world. Both these conceptions, however, interpret the relation between God and the world with people in it as a *cosmological* relation; in both conceptions, God is a proper object of human intentions, a being. By being other than the person intending, God in this view relativizes rather than absolutizes the intender.

There is another approach to the problem of God in Western thought which does find God in the absolute experience of things. Paul Tillich distinguished the two approaches in the following way:

One can distinguish two ways of approaching God: the way of overcoming estrangement and the way of meeting a stranger. In the first way man discovers *himself* when he discovers God; he discovers something that is identical with himself although it transcends him infinitely, something from which he is estranged, but from which he never has been and never can be separated. In the second way man meets a *stranger* when he meets God. . . . The two ways symbolize the two possible types of philosophy of religion: the ontological type and the cosmological type. The way of overcoming estrangement symbolizes the ontological method in the philosophy of religion. The way of meeting a stranger symbolizes the cosmological method.[4]

According to the ontological approach, God is closer to us than we are to ourselves, particularly when we are lost in our intentions elsewhere. God is not a separate being but the Being in each person, for Tillich. To claim that Tillich's thought exhibits the distinction between the relative and the absolute is not to show that his theory provides a theology adequate for either philosophical or religious purposes. Yet it does demonstrate that the distinction between relative and absolute as two respects in which finite things can be regarded is close to the heart of a major Western sense of the spiritual quest.

Spiritual development concerns the way in which people should take possession of their own existence. It is not directly an ideal for the kind of existence which they should have; personal and social freedoms are ideals for kinds of existence, as are justice, beauty, and many other excellences. Spiritual freedom deals, rather, with the way in which people should relate to the existence which they do have. It supposes as a problem the common situation in which people can be alienated from what they are, even when in objective terms their existence is successful and should be "happy." There are examples of people with great achievements in autonomy and social participation who still are not "present" in their own lives, who feel estranged from their own successes. There are also examples of people who live according to the wills of others, with neither personal autonomy nor social effectiveness, and yet who are at peace and possessed of tremendous inner strength. Spiritual freedom is an ideal which addresses the fact that people can be alienated from their own existence, or perfectly present in the poorest existence. This is not to suggest that spiritual freedom is not aided by the advantages of personal and social freedom, as well as by justice, beauty, and many other values. But it does suggest that spiritual freedom is an ideal for a different dimension of life, for what may be called the ontological dimension.

The spiritual models of the soldier, sage, and saint, then, have to do with those elements of psychic integrity, enlightenment, and perfection of the heart which bear upon the immediate or absolute aspect of existence. The integrity of the soldier, for instance, is not necessarily the same as the autonomy of personal freedom; indeed, the soldier may be under the orders of another. It has to do, rather, with the capacity to integrate all one's forces wholly to be present in thought and action; in this sense, one must be one's own master before one can give oneself over to the orders of another, if that should ever be required. The enlightenment of the sage is not exactly wisdom about the world, but about the absolute meaning of such wisdom. Perfection of the heart is not merely the problem of strengthening the right desires and abandoning the bad ones, but doing so precisely as a matter of affirming one's own identity and existence, of "choosing life."

The ontological dimension of life has generally been associated with religion, which accounts for the association of spirituality with religion. Where ontology has been taken to imply reference to an absolute object, the religion has been theistic; where it has been taken to imply the absence of such an object, as in Buddhism, the religion has been atheistic. Belief in God as such is not definitive of religion; neither is concern for spiritual development. It is necessary now to consider just what the relation is between religion and spiritual development.

RELIGIONS, THE SPIRITUAL, AND THE RELIGIOUS

I

The general collapse of the world's religions decisively shaped the problems of our times. When they were whole and vital, the religions which arose out of China, India, and the Mideast-European cultures nurtured three human concerns generally taken to be fundamental. Through *ritual* they shaped people's actions so that action is not merely "doing" but "taking possession of the world." Through their symbolic and conceptual *cosmologies* they provided an interpretation of the world in terms of which people could share basic values and construe the hard facts of life—life, death, destruction, suffering, and the passage of time—as having human or even cosmic meaning. Through their devotional practices they provided methods and symbolic contexts for the *spiritual development* of individuals so that they could be "present" in the world with integrity and sincerity.

Those three concerns are indeed primordial and necessary components of human experience, as the following chapters will demonstrate in part. Actions, of course, can be conceived as merely the redistribution of matter; but this conception is divorced from meaning in human experience. Action can also be conceived as work for the sake of some value—bringing food to the mouth, dancing a perfect movement. But these "works" provide definition of the human place in the world, a problem of absolute rather than of only instrumental existence, when they are experienced in terms of mythical, symbolic, or conceptual cosmologies of the world and human life. It is not enough to have the actions and the symbols separately; the actions must be experienced in terms of the symbols, and this is the role of ritual.

Necessary too are the cosmologies, what Peter Berger calls the "sacred canopies." Human experience seeks not only meaningful action but meanings which may be thought about and enjoyed as such. Furthermore, it is up to each individual to come to terms with himself or herself as one who acts and finds meaning; over and above the effectiveness of action or the validity of meanings, individual spiritual development is the task which each person has of relating himself or herself absolutely to the concerns of life.

When religions were whole, they provided life forms which more or less integrated the needs for ritual, cosmology, and personal spiritual development. Those needs obviously refer to and indeed imply each other in some sense. But with the breakdown of the religions in the twentieth century, those needs are being pursued in somewhat separate areas of human endeavor.

Of course, it is something of an oversimplification to say that the world's religions have collapsed. Many people still identify themselves through membership in them, and most religions still have some economic and political power, particularly in the West and Mideast. There is no reason to doubt that for some people the piety in any of the world's great religions is as sincere and vital as it ever was. Furthermore, the leading thinkers in the great traditions seem to be able to defend the essential intent of their rituals to their own satisfaction, to make clear the basic truths of their theologies, and to justify even the most esoteric spiritual practices to those who are interested—all this against the criticisms of the anti-religious secular intellectual world.

The question inevitably arises whether civilization can do without religion. On the one hand, people who are literate and who have access to the vast technologies of communication may well be able to partake of religious traditions in a satisfactory way without belonging to religions. On the other hand, many people without the interest in and capacity to appropriate initially alien cultures may need institutions exerting efforts on their behalf. Surely much of the structure of organized religions has had to do with educational and culture-conveying functions which may now be more authentically performed by other structures. I regard this as an open question and make no prediction about whether present cultural upheavals may lead to new forms which may legitimately be identified as religions.

I believe, however, that at least one aspect of traditional religions will and should fall prey to a decisive moral argument. Among their other functions, religions have provided a group identity for people, a sense of belonging. But there is a moral problem here: belonging to a religious tradition seems to imply a distinction between those who belong and those who do not, between the Chosen People and the gentiles. A more primitive sense of belonging was associated perhaps with tribal identity; religious belonging supplanted or at least came to compete with this in the areas affected by the rise of the great urban universal religions in the centuries around the time of Christ. But the implication of the very universality in those religions has morally undermined the sense of belonging characteristic of either tribal or religious identity. The moral problem is this: How can I, as a member of a (tribal or) religious group, have such openness of heart with someone who is not a member of my group that I can be his or her brother? This is an intensely practical problem. The very conditions of open communication entail an openness to being persuaded to the other person's position; there can be no stand upon a prior commitment which reduces the other person to an object, an outsider who need not be considered, if communication is to be open, truly dialectical. Yet can Jews and Christians have genuine communication? Each can honestly tell the other about their commitments, of course, but can they do more than share experiences?

For all its shallowness, the eighteenth-century Enlightenment was correct in seeing that reason is universal and that anything which causes arbitrary separation is immoral, disrespective of the outsiders as "ends in themselves." Reason is perhaps too abstract a term; "process of communication" is better. The difficulty with the Enlightenment was that its conception of reason seemed not to hold the living waters of experience and tradition. Surely communication about experience and inherited tradition is among the most important kinds of communication. But any experience or tradition which requires a person to be unresponsive to the appeals or arguments of another is no longer living but dead, and deadening. Is not religious tradition, including spiritual tradition, just such a deadening factor? Has not the history of religious thinking been mainly apologetical, justifying why the thinker stands where he does rather than engage in dialogue with another?

Because of these considerations many sensitive secular people shrink from discussions of "spiritual" matters, objecting not to the content, but to the language which carries religious associations distinguishing between those who are in and those who are out, and defining people by objective belonging rather than by subjective interchange. Universal morality entails that the exclusiveness of religious identification be immoral.

Two responses can be made to this. One is that the spiritual traditions, indeed the religious traditions at large, are not parts of the *human* tradition. They should be allowed to identify people as belonging not to exclusive groups but to the inclusive human group.

The other response is more subtle, and it involves recognition of human will. In an open discussion, the participants not only exchange information but also respond to the information and to each other in many volitional ways. Now, it may well be, and often is, that one participant responds to the thoroughly shared information and personal presentations differently from other participants, willing a different moral course, assessing values differently, appropriating different elements to be important to his or her own experience. Openness of communication *requires* that volitional differences of this sort be possible. Does this not mean that it is then morally possible for people to choose paths which take them apart and cut off further communication? If so, may they not then choose to belong to different religious groups, viewing the others as having made wrong choices?

This is an extremely difficult problem, one which cannot be tackled in any depth here. To suggest an answer, I would say that on the moral level the basic condition is to respect the integrity of those with whom one communicates. This entails allowing them to break off communication if they choose to do so, but it also entails that one not break off communication oneself because to do so would be to objectify the others as merely being members of the "other" group. Furthermore, morality gives license, I believe, always to argue to others that they *should not* break off communication, even though they have the right to choose to do so. These points are part of the conception of the moral community which Kant described so well. But, as Kierkegaard pointed out, perhaps religions make claims transcending morality. Perhaps; and perhaps not.

The argument can be turned around. If, for instance, everyone should be interested, to some degree or another, in psychic integrity, and everyone should participate in dialogue with interested parties, and if the religious and spiritual traditions have something to say about psychic integrity, then everyone has the obligation to engage the experience of those traditions, and of those who make that experience alive.

The above discussion warrants drawing an important distinction, however, between historical religions and certain religious elements of civilization. The religious elements—the needs for ritual, cosmology, and spiritual development, for instance—may under some circumstances be properly met in institutional religions. In other circumstances the religions might not meet those needs. To the extent that those needs are legitimate, this failure would stand as a criticism of the religions, and indeed the prophets of the Bible were adept at voicing such criticism. When religions do not fulfill the religious functions, societies tend to seek out other cultural means. It then becomes something of a semantic problem to determine whether those needs should still be called religious. To do so is to call attention to the cultural continuity of the needs and the resources which the religious traditions might offer to other arenas of experience. Our present situation, I believe, is one in which the basic religious needs for ritual, cosmology, and spiritual development are being pursued outside the context of religions. Because of the close association of the models of soldier, sage, and saint with the traditions of the great religions, it is helpful to set the context for the present discussion by mentioning the religious arenas outside religions.[5]

II

It appears that the contemporary stage for significant action, and for the rituals which epitomize it, is politics. Politics has always been something of a religion in America, and political, particularly revolutionary, action has supplanted religious action as the arena which most of the world's populations (as represented by their elites) feel contains humanly significant action.

If it is true that the action deserving of demarcation in ritual is that action by which people establish their relation to the world as significant actors, one can see why religions ritualized the actions which they did. In primeval times the actions which were decisive were those which provided food: whence the animal and vegetation fertility rituals. In the ages when food was produced for a burgeoning population by means of the organization of labor under the direction of hierarchical authority, significant action was the recognition of lordship: the Chinese Lord of Heaven, the Indian Lord Krishna, the Hebrew Lord of Hosts are all celebrated in rituals as "bosses" with might to assert organizing authority. In the great period of worldwide urbanization and imperial social organization, extending for three hundred years before and after the lifetime of Jesus, the problem of the masses included dislocation from the countryside into large cities with unfamiliar "common" languages and a feeling that life was determined by social (not natural) forces which somehow claim ownership. Significant action then was to establish a meaning to life based, not on lost connections with the countryside or on enslaving social relations, but on universal properties of human life; and rituals celebrated the individual cultivation of the universal human spirit which would in turn redeem individuals from the social pawnshop. This intense combination of personal cultivation and commitment to the thesis, absurd as it must have seemed at the time, that poor individuals, without direct political power, could reform society characterized the rituals of Han Confucianism, Mahāyāna Buddhism, and Christianity, the great religions taking shape during that period. The world's religions did not so much supplant the rituals of earlier times as overlay them with new dimensions of significant actions, a process which has continued to the present day.

To hazard a generalization: significant action today seems to center in developing and reinforcing the forms of social organization which distribute goods on the basis of community decision rather than on the decision of particular groups within the community. This is not to say that basic production and distribution are not still problems, or that authority within social organization is not a problem, but only that they are subsumed under the larger and more urgent problem: communal decision making. This problem is manifest in the developing countries, the Marxist and socialist countries, and in the tensions over capitalism in the Western European and American countries. People seem most alive when addressing these problems, and in The People's Republic of China, where they have been addressed most consistently and thoroughly, there seem to be new rituals arising.[6]

The roots of much of the concern for communal politics as the domain for significant human action lie in religion, particularly Protestant Christianity. Robert Bellah has discussed the founding American Puritan myth as developing a strict regard for individual responsibility with a community based on ultimate moral or religious imperatives. He quotes John Winthrop's sermon "A Modell of Christian Charity," which says that for the end of establishing a successful community in America in covenant with God,

> Wee must be knitt together in this worke as one man, wee must entertaine each other in brotherly Affeccion, wee must be willing to abridge our selves of our superflueities, for the supply of others necessities, wee must uphold a familiar Commerce together in all meeknes, gentleness, patience and liberallity, wee must delight in each other, make others Condicions our owne, rejoyce together, mourne together, labour and suffer together, allwayes haveing before our eyes our Commission and Community in the worke. . . .[7]

The sermon goes on to say that when these conditions are met, ten of the colonists will be able to resist a thousand of their enemies and their city will be set as a light upon the hill for all to see and emulate. That sounds like a quaint translation of a speech of the late Chairman Mao!

Not all people with visions of social reorganization are in situations similar to those of the Puritans or of the Chinese, and can have realistic hopes of founding a completely new society. But there are models for authentic political action within the limits of a larger intractable and unjust society which derive from religion. For instance, John Wesley long before Marx recognized the personal alienation resulting from economic enslavement, and organized his revolution among the poor working class of England to meet the problem. His "congregations" were not parishes competing with the established Anglican church but "classes," small groups of people who met weekly or oftener for Bible reading, mutual support, and, most importantly, mutual criticism in the sense practiced by contemporary Marxist "cells." Unlike the Puritans, who demanded proof of conversion before inclusion within the covenanted community, the Methodists took in anyone whom they could persuade to come, and worked to transform individual characters through communal appeals to individual responsibility. This acceptance of everyone, along with a method of "conversion" which recognizes autonomy, seems to be a condition for any genuine social revolution.

For whatever reasons—perhaps parochialism and a lack of recognition of the overall economic structures which must be changed—the organized religions have not sufficiently nourished those roots, which grew instead in other soil. The concern to identify and epitomize in ritual certain actions as the prime bearers of humanly significant relation to the world is always a religious concern. But religions are not the only loci of religious concerns, and in the present time it seems that it is in political action that the religious concern for ritually important action is to be found.

Besides ritual actions religions have also provided cosmologies which interpret the world as a whole, indicate its unconditional features, and depict
a place for mankind with values which define success in occupying that
place. The cosmologies have employed myths, symbols, and extensive systems of interpretation, related in various ways to each other according to
social context and population. Whatever the conceptual form, these cosmologies have sometimes been broad enough and systematic enough to provide people with a sense for classifying the relative importance of elements
in their world, and deep and emotion-laden enough to do this on all levels
of consciousness.

The rise of modern science has been enough to take the authority out of
the old religious cosmologies. Those cosmologies did not sufficiently distinguish between claims of empirical fact and the "deeper" religious truths
which they contained. Furthermore, they were tied to social symbols
which simply are not alive today: God the king can be *only* a symbol now,
and something which is appreciated as "only" a symbol cannot grip a society with enough power to be an authoritative cosmology. Theologians
in the West during this century have been concerned to demythologize the
religions' cosmologies, distinguishing the mythic truth from the mythic
trappings, and making the whole compatible with empirical science and
current social goals. However much there is a valid mythic truth to the old
cosmologies, the old cosmologies do not present themselves in a form in
which they can be appropriated by those in touch with today's currents.
Ricoeur is doubtless correct in saying that the only way to grasp the fundamental realities is through the historical demythologizing of the myths,
but the resulting historical understanding is not the grasping of the truths
itself.[8] In China, the ancient cosmologies are believed to be incompatible
with the current social needs and rejected outright, as has been evident in
the attack on Confucianism; only the empirical folklore is preserved.

Our age no less than any other needs a cosmology for coherence, for
social and personal guidance, and for the possibility of community. It also
needs a cosmology which can make sense of its needed rituals and forms
of spiritual development. The old cosmologies all have valuable resources
to provide in terms of myths, symbols, and interpretive conceptions. But
if they are to be helpful they must be taken up in a form which also critically incorporates science and contemporary social realities. A viable contemporary cosmology seems to require several levels. On one level, it must
be expressible in a clear conceptual form which can be subjected to philosophical criticism. On another level, those concepts must be transformed
into the images which can form basic experience and be moved by such
experience. The cosmology should be an operative guide for organizing
the social community, at the same time as it is continually reformed by the
experience of that community. Since the current community is a *world*
community, in senses which will be discussed later, a viable contemporary

cosmology should employ and reflect upon the cultures of all the peoples of the world if it is to be respectful.

That our world has no viable cosmology now is commonly recognized. Some philosophers argue that, however much one is wanted, a cosmology of this sort is impossible, itself an artifact of bygone religions. But others take the construction of a cosmology to be the central philosophic task of our time. It can well be argued that philosophy has now finally come of age, taking over from organized religious institutions the task of providing, continually revising, and reforming a socially viable cosmology. To do this, philosophy will have to cultivate systematic speculative talents, establish cordial and sympathetic channels of communication with the sciences and other disciplines, and base itself on the historical resources of the world's major cultural traditions. Although most Anglo-Saxon philosophers do not think of the task in this way, the task itself defines the discipline. The discipline is philosophy, however, and not religious apologetics. The task may be religious in the sense of addressing the ancient religious concerns, but its pursuit now takes place most often and profoundly in a domain independent of the world's organized religions.

IV

Personal spiritual development has always been intimately related to everything people do, including their significant humanizing actions and their understanding. Furthermore, the collapse of the world's religions is least manifest in the domain of spiritual development. Within the Western world, at least, there seems to be a resurgence of interest in religious techniques of spiritual life, not only through imported Asian religions but also in monastic, pentecostal, and cabalistic traditions of the West. Nevertheless, with the weakening of the institutional, ritualistic, and theological components of religion, the spiritual exercises have become *techniques*, methods of attaining spiritual ends. This is evident, for instance, in the parallel between spiritual techniques and psychoanalysis and related psychological technologies. Herbert Fingarette's brilliant *The Self in Transformation* develops these parallels in a profound way, arguing that there is an unusual affinity between psychoanalysis and certain Eastern conceptions of the spiritual problem and of the goals of "therapy." Furthermore, recent developments in biology and psychology have made some of the spiritual techniques, such as those in yoga, seem more legitimate to Westerners. It is in the area of spiritual development, more than in ritual or cosmology, that contemporary secular points of view tend to coalesce with traditional religious ones.

The context in which I want to examine the ancient models of the soldier, sage, and saint is one in which it may be presumed that any contemporary person can stand. Although spiritual development, historically speaking, is a religious problem, it does not entail belonging to a religion; it is even compatible with hostility to religion as long as that hostility allows for taking certain demythologized elements of traditions seriously. On the other hand, it does not preclude commitments to a religious or ethnic group so long as these do not entail excluding the resources of *other* religious traditions. The condition making this study relevant to religious believers, religious abstainers, and those hostile to religion is the same: readiness to penetrate and appropriate the experiences central to the world's religious traditions whenever these are valuable and relevant. Why this is so occupies the discussion of the final section of this chapter.

THE HUMAN TRADITION

Our resources for understanding spiritual development through the models of soldier, sage, and saint include a great many spiritual traditions. From the standpoint of many people who have been raised within the Western spiritual heritage, and who have not bothered to penetrate through its inherited disguises to the core, the hope for spiritual liberation often seems to lie outside the West. Enthusiasms for Hindu, Buddhist, and Taoist teachers and writings, for "primitive" paths to salvation such as that of Don Juan in Castaneda's saga, and for the occult "sciences" rejected by the West, are surely fads. But they are well-founded ones! There are immense spiritual resources in these traditions which should be appropriated in thorough and serious ways. The energy in the fads should be harnessed to the disciplines required to appropriate those traditions.

The shallowness of the faddish interest in non-Western spiritual traditions rests on three principal points. The first is that they seem to give the promise of rescuing Westerners from their human problems without requiring them to face those problems. They seem to say that those problems are somehow either unreal or, in the case of occultism, in the control of forces other than human. This part of the fad is a desire to escape responsibility. But there is no genuine spiritual tradition which warrants the escape from responsibility. In fact, most *increase* the scope of things for which one is to be responsible: the saint is responsible even for the urgings of his heart! A more thorough understanding of the traditions would put this faddish element to rest.

The second reason for the fad is a desire for an easy technology to attain psychic integrity. But no spiritual path is easy or quick; the paths of instant enlightenment may reach the omega quickly enough, but the problem is to stay there. One of the signs of faddishness in the cult of non-Western spirituality is the frequent switching from one path to another. Initial experiences that life includes things which Western science has not dreamed of are often insufficient to sustain people through the long haul of a serious spiritual path and do not provide the proper motivation anyway.

The third reason is that the non-Western spiritual traditions simply are not present in the West in a congenial way for Westerners. It is almost as if Westerners need to become something other than Western to employ those other spiritual resources. This is partly the fault of insufficient scholarship. American colleges and universities too often teach culture as if the primitives, India, and China were appendices. Not enough books have been translated well. There are not enough teachers for whom the non-Western traditions live. There are few models in the West for appropriating the other traditions. As a consequence it seems as if Westerners must adopt Indian or Chinese culture to learn from their spiritual traditions. And because few can switch cultures in any but the most superficial way, the whole effort hardly leaves the faddish stage.

The cultural and philosophic problem here is that of appropriating a heritage. All those born into a society are given something of a heritage willy-nilly. But what they receive as given is fairly shallow. To deepen their possession of a heritage, people must actively take it up, appropriate it. The question then becomes which heritage or heritages to take up. It is clear that when the possession of a heritage moves from a passive to an active mode the viable elements of culture include more than those merely given by everyday socialization.

"Higher education" in many respects can be taken as the institution of society providing the resources of human experience which can be taken up by those actively appropriating a heritage beyond the immediate culture. So colleges make available the experiences of Western civilization. But what about other traditions? Sometimes it is argued that the Western tradition constitutes people in the West, and that they must appropriate it first before turning to the alien cultures. But that supposes an absurd view of cultural determinism, as if one's genes determine one's culture. If the scholarly resources regarding the other traditions were available, those traditions could be appropriated along with the Western ones whenever relevant and compatible with the rest of life.

The "relevance" of resources depends, not on direct past historical causation, but on the needs of people living in the present. Of course, the present is determined by past factors, but not necessarily in ways which provide for exclusive relevance of specific past cultures. It may well be, for instance, that the causal development of Western culture has provided only shallow spiritual resources to the twentieth century, and that the only profound resources for Westerners' problems must come from outside. That is a superficial judgment, of course, since the spiritual resources of Judaism, Christianity, and Islam seem to look as profound from Eastern perspectives as the other way around. But it probably is the case that for many educated Western people now the depths of the Western spiritual traditions are better appreciated in connection with non-Western spiritual traditions than in connection with present Western science and its ideology.

The relation between a society and the cultures providing its civilized resources can be conceived in something like the following way. The scope of a society is determined by the configurations of causal interactions between people, individually and in groups. Thus, people or groups are within the same society if they interact in socially meaningful ways. Several groups of people, therefore, can be in the same society, although each derives from its own unique cultural heritage. Given the conditions of modern technology, economics, political and military affairs, and travel, most of the world is rather well integrated into one society, under this consideration.

As to culture, any social group ought to attend to and appropriate for its own resources the heritages of all the groups with which it interacts. This is a "principle of relevant cultures." Not to observe it is to involve a group in treating other groups as less than human, because their civilizing cultures are ignored and they are judged according to one's own group's everyday heritage.

But it is not only immoral to fail to appropriate the cultures of others, it is stupid. Cultures are resources for deepening and enlightening one's own experience; they are resources for acting with more options, more vision, and more steadfastness. But the situations for which cultures are relevant resources are always present situations. If by some pre-established harmony the present situation faced by any group were always one for which the culture associated with its unique historical development were sufficient, it would be satisfactory to attend only to the culture of one's parents. But the extent of a group's present situation is defined by the scope of the society throughout which it interacts. Precisely because the present situation for groups today involves them in interaction with groups whose cultural parents are different, no group should limit its actively appropriated heritage to that associated with its own historical development. An American's situation is determined by the historical development of the East as well as that of the West. Not to see this is to force perception into needlessly parochial molds.

Therefore, it is time to speak of the *human tradition*, not the Western tradition or the Chinese or the Indian tradition as if these could stand usefully by themselves. The human tradition consists of all those cultures which might relevantly be appropriated by any group in our common society. From this perspective an historical understanding of the human tradition can be far more sensitive and accurate than the historical approaches seeking to view the whole from the standpoint of a single strand. There are interconnections and parallels often missed by the parochial approaches which stand out in the broader perspective.

Appropriation of a tradition, of course, does not mean accepting it as unqualifiedly valid for one's present situation. Rather, it means coming to terms with the tradition in a human way, accepting some elements and rejecting others. More accurately put: appropriation begins by coming to understand a tradition's way of being human and then deciding how that historically bears on one's own situation. Elements are not so much accepted or rejected as given some measure of importance in one's own life —perhaps different from the measure they received in the past. One may accept something as "valid still today," but only by combining it with other elements unique to today, combinations which could not have existed in the past. People attentive to present existence will appoint their lives with those cultural forms most relevant to their own situation. The spiritual discipline of ancient Indian yoga, for instance, may be much more viable today than its parallel in Western chivalry because of its compatibility with contemporary science; medieval chivalry seems too intimately intertwined with a religious cosmology alien to contemporary experience. For one group to appropriate another's historical heritage is not to accept it as normative, but to understand it as human, historically definitive of the other group in some measure, and perhaps as relevant for the appointment of one's own social style.

No American can become a Hindu as the Indians can be Hindus. It would mean the alienation of the American from native American culture (something impossible for an Indian). No American past the age of infancy can pick up the everyday Indian culture automatically passed on to Indian infants. But this is not to say that Americans cannot be converts, and vice versa. A convert is a strange member of a culture precisely because he or she has picked it up voluntarily and in necessarily abstract ways. History is full of conversions, particularly spiritual conversions. Necessarily a synthesizer, a convert may change from one name to another, but he or she is always a mixture of both. When this is recognized, sensitive attention can be given to the process of synthesizing cultures well. Instead of worrying about maintaining the purity of Western cultures, or even their primacy—a very dangerous idea indeed—the worry should be to enrich one culture with another. Syncretistic opportunities need not be shallow but can be creative.

After all the apologia for cultural syncretism, it still must be recognized that each person's identity is expressed historically, not culturally. People are defined not by congeries of cultural elements, purely inherited or syncretistically composed, but by the paths of their developing acculturation and action. History, not culture, reveals the *choices* which people make in forming their own identities, including choices about which cultures to appropriate. No matter how much Americans and Europeans appropriate of non-Western cultures, they will always be Americans or Europeans who have done that. This will change the contours of Western culture, but only by changing the identity of that tradition itself. After a while it may no longer be relevant to identify ourselves as Westerners or Easterners; perhaps that time has already come. But even should we attain with the Indians and Chinese, for instance, a common appropriation of the human tradition, they would be Easterners who have done that, and we Westerners.

The three chapters immediately following will present models of the spiritual soldier, the sage, and the saint, exploring the spiritual dimensions of each. There are three kinds of control on the truth of the arguments to come. The first is a formal requirement that the models be based on dialectically defensible philosophical categories, and that the speculative conceptions be coherent. The second is an empirical requirement that the various dimensions of spiritual development cited be reasonably faithful to the traditions of experience out of which they come; even if a person rejects the task of spiritual liberation, the argument here urges his or her assent as to what that would be in the light of the experiences of the human tradition. The following discussions make no claim to have interpreted *all* aspects of spiritual development, of course, only those of principal importance in three models. The third control is the pragmatic requirement that the models present relevant ideals which would genuinely enrich life. Because much of the intrinsic value of such goals can be appreciated only when the goals have been deliberately adopted, and in fact derive value from the adoption, the results of the pragmatic control are hard to measure publicly.

NOTES

1. Analects 2:4, in *A Sourcebook in Chinese Philosophy*, ed. and trans. Wingtsit Chan (Princeton: Princeton University Press, 1963). Information concerning authors or works to which reference but no direct citation is made in the text will be found in the bibliography.

2. An underlying intent of this book is to demonstrate how a certain kind of norm may be justified. There are, of course, many kinds of alleged norms, including character ideals of the sort discussed here, moral rules, personal and social goals, policy norms, and the like; the present discussion deals with only one kind. My aim here is to demonstrate justification, not to talk about it.

3. "Cosmology" here means the study, or the conceptual result of such a study, of the first principles describing this world in terms of which all elements of experience can be interpreted as illustrations. Alfred North Whitehead, for instance, is a modern cosmologist in this sense, although some of the ancient mythologies were also cosmologies in primitive versions of this sense. The important transfer of cosmology from religion to philosophy will be discussed in the following section.

4. "The Two Types of Philosophy of Religion," in *Theology of Culture*, ed. Robert Kimball (New York: Oxford University Press, 1959), p. 10.

5. For purposes of orientation, this section makes certain large-scale generalizations concerning religion in history. Although always false in detail, the overall drift of the generalizations is, I believe, valid in each case. Aside from the particular works cited, readers might compare these generalizations with William McNeill's *The Rise of the West* (Chicago: The University of Chicago Press, 1963) and with Sidney E. Ahlstrom's *A Religious History of the American People* (New Haven: Yale University Press, 1972). Geoffrey Barraclough's *An Introduction to Contemporary History* (Baltimore: Penguin, 1967) may also be of interest.

6. For a detailed account of the effects of revolution on the rituals, cosmology, and spiritual development of a village, see William Hinton's *Fanshen* (New York: Vintage, 1966).

7. In *The Broken Covenant: American Civil Religion in Time of Trial* (New York: Seabury, 1975), p. 14.

8. Ricoeur writes of the modern consciousness: "In every way, something has been lost, irremediably lost: immediacy of belief. But if we can no longer live the great symbolisms of the sacred in accordance with the original belief in them, we can, we modern men, aim at a second naïveté in and through criti-

cism. . . . As an advance post of 'modernity' criticism cannot help being a 'demythologization'; that is, an irreversible gain of truthfulness, of intellectual honesty, and therefore of objectivity. But it is precisely because it accelerates the movement of 'demythologization' that modern hermeneutics brings to light the dimension of the symbol, as a primordial sign of the sacred; it is thus that it participates in the revivification of philosophy through contact with symbols; it is one of the ways of rejuvenating philosophy" (*The Symbolism of Evil*, trans. Emerson Buchanan [Boston: Beacon, 1969], pp. 351–53).

2

The Soldier

IN SPIRITUAL MATTERS license is the opposite of freedom. "Free spirits," variously swayed by their senses and passions, by ringing appeals and visions, may be free in many ways; but they are not free in spirit. Psychic integrity is the root of spiritual freedom, and psychic integrity begins in discipline.

Spiritual discipline is paradoxical, however. At first it looks like the building of an improved and more integrated self, one more independent and uniquely defined than the ordinary personality. Discipline aims to tie the self together, rendering it more sensitive to its surroundings but at the same time less susceptible to being swayed involuntarily. Psychic integrity rests on a highly developed will, and will is what most distinguishes one person from another.

The seeker discovers the paradox soon enough. Jesus warned: "One who grasps at self will lose it, but one who rejects self on my account will gain it" (Mt 10:39; see also Mt 16:25). This principle is echoed in the Hindu emphasis on detachment, in Buddhism's denial of the substantiality of the self, and in Taoism's injunction to be one with the tao. Confucianism appears to offer unrelieved advocacy of the Superior Person; but, although the language betrays an important difference in emphasis, the Superior Person must still be sincere, and this means being transparent to the depths of his or her being and utterly responsive to external demands without the interposition of a misleading self-image. In short, spiritual discipline requires and leads to the abandonment and dissolution of the self!

To understand the heroic development of spiritual soldiers thoroughly is impossible from a theoretical point of view. A theory can only lay out standard contexts and stages of growth. Yet, in large measure, heroes are formed by unique and historically contingent events in which they create their will by exercising it. No hero can be educated according to a program planned in advance, as Jesuits and Methodists—religious groups with military metaphors—have discovered. Yet a theoretical discussion of the stages of growth can indicate the general contours of becoming a spiritual soldier.

The first and most basic component or instrument of psychic integrity is will. The education of the spirited part of the soul, to use Plato's phrase, results in a good will. But what is will? The history of Western civilization has shown this to be a baffling question indeed. Will, cognition, and desire are so intricately intertwined that metaphors suggesting compartmentalization will not serve to distinguish them. Nor can they be viewed as separate operations on common contents, as may be suggested in saying that desire presents an object, cognition understands it, and the will affirms. Rather, they must be conceived as different dimensions of a unitary process of life, cultivated by different activities, perhaps shifting in relative importance at different times.

Will may be conceived as that dimension of human life having to do with marshaling all the inherited and perceived components of experience, including bodily structures, into a unified, individual, public expression. The *resources* of the will are all the components to be unified. The *effectiveness* of the will consists in the fact that future events will have to take account of the way one comports oneself as the result of the unifying process. The *purposiveness* in will lies in the fact that the unifying process aims at some pattern which will in fact make the components compatible in a desired definite way relevant for the context of action. Of course, part of the process of will is arriving at such a unifying pattern; this is to say, will is not merely action according to purpose but also the establishment of that purpose. Some aspects of will are conscious, particularly those depending on cognitive deliberations about purposes. But since Freud (indeed since Plato —see *Republic*, Bk VIII) we know that much of will is not conscious.

The importance of will—hence, its primacy in spiritual development—is an ontological matter. Self-integration is not merely one among the many things one does. One's very existence is one's continual self-integration. Although psychic integrity—one's spiritual status—is always relative to particular components to be integrated and particular purposes to be served, the process of integration itself, the exercise of will, is one's very "act of existence."

That the process of integration is personal existence as such is something claimed by theory, and it is typical of any theory such as Plato's or Whitehead's which represents the self as social. A social theory of self claims that there are diverse components of the self which are integrated through the activity of pursuing a coordinating ideal, to the extent that they are integrated at all. The life of a self is necessarily processive and defined by both the components to be integrated and the pattern of ideals pursued. The alternative theory is that the self is a substance, unified by a fixed inner core with only its aspects changing. Substantial change is, at most, the development of previously fixed potentials in the face of the contingencies of the environment (Aristotle), or the maintenance of the self (Spinoza's *conatus*) in such an environment. The social theory, however, makes better sense of the tenuousness of experience.

Everyone exercises will in this broad sense; otherwise one would not exist. But most of us have not attended to will as such and use the concept to interpret only the situations in which we face problems. Only in crisis situations in which we face momentous decisions or formidable obstacles are we generally aware of willing at all or of the difference between willing well and willing poorly. (Willing well is very close to being well, and vice versa.) For the ordinary demands of social life, this is enough; if it were not, society would require more explicit attention to discipline than it does.

Spiritual soldiers are people who single out for explicit attention and development the concerns of the will. Like military men who drill and perfect their capacity to handle weapons in advance of fighting, who develop their character to be courageous and steadfast in battle, and loyal to their orders, spiritual soldiers purify their will by attending to it in some conscious distinction from the relative affairs of life.

In experience as well as in the literature of the human tradition, there are four levels of will to be purified beyond ordinary development: will in one's self-image, in one's action, in one's consciousness, and in one's devotion. In the purification of self-image, psychic integrity seems mostly to be the *assertion* of oneself; in the purification of devotion it seems mostly to be the *abandonment* of self. Self-image, action, consciousness, and devotion are not themselves identical with will. Discipline is, rather, the perfection of the will—that is, the integrating activity—as it is expressed in them all.

According to the philosophic construct sketched in the previous chapter, another set of variables is to be considered in connection with the levels of self-image, action, consciousness, and devotion. Each of those levels involves some comportment of *desires* according to some structure subject to *reason*. Since desires and reason are coordinated by *spirit*, each of the levels of spiritual development is to be analyzed according to its disposition of spirit, desires, and reason.

PURIFICATION OF WILL IN SELF-IMAGE

The foundation for any explicit attention to the development of will is one's self-image. One cannot realistically begin to deal with perfecting psychic integrity until one becomes aware of who one believes oneself to be. And then one must develop a proper image of oneself as capable of spiritual development on one's own responsibility, no matter what help one seeks or receives. Spiritual soldiers must come to terms with the image they hold of themselves de facto, correct it to one of which they approve, and assert it as the guiding principle of their spiritual development. Despite the fact that higher stages of psychic integrity require the elimination of narcissism and even of any sense of ego, the process of development is corrupted from the beginning if one lacks a sense of confidence in one's own ability, feels determined and contained by parents or other significant figures, and excuses one's major actions as being someone else's responsibility or the result of environment, heredity, or age.

One of the most interesting lessons of psychoanalysis has been that the self-image which one truly has and according to which one acts is often quite different from the conscious image one tells oneself that one has. One may come on with confidence, assertiveness, and bluster, thinking oneself the take-charge leader. But the analyst can quickly show that one really believes oneself insecure and threatened by the initiative of others, or perhaps terrified that one will be forgotten if one is not the center of attention.

A crucial beginning of psychic integrity is getting in touch, and coming to terms, with basic self-images. This is not the same as discovering one's true desires and fears, although they are related. It is, rather, discovering how one feels oneself to be defined by those desires and fears. The major spiritual traditions have introspective techniques for calling forth and coming to terms with the unconscious components of self-image, tantric elements of Eastern traditions being the most obvious. Psychoanalysis is perhaps the most efficient for Westerners attuned to science.

From the standpoint of spiritedness or psychic integrity, the question with regard to one's self-image is whether one feels oneself to be free. (From the standpoint of reason, the question is whether one's image is true to oneself; from the standpoint of desires, the question is whether the image is a fulfilling one.) Of all the kinds of bondage, from chains through ignorance to perverted enfranchisement, the most pathetic is the belief in oneself as incompetent, as dependent, as non-responsible. Spiritual soldiers develop a discipline which gives them images of themselves as independent agents capable of responsible will.

One's image of one's own spirit has to do with confidence that one can in fact exert will. This is not the same as confidence that one can perform this or that action, command this or that loyalty or love. The basic question is whether one feels oneself to be capable of will generally. Of course, if one exists, one is necessarily "willing" in the broad sense. But one may not know this or may feel instead that one's will is merely an extension of the wills of others. One may feel that the principles according to which one wills are not expressive of one's own personality. The result is not only that one is in fact bound to others or to chaos, but that one does not exist at the human level of being one's own person; one exists only as a human organism organized according to principles other than fully personal ones.

If one lacks an image of oneself as capable of willing, how can it be acquired? The answer is, by the assertion of one's own will! That, of course, may not be what self-denying people want to hear. Like Dumbo they want a magic feather to enable them to fly. How can one will oneself to feel able to will when one feels unable in the first place?

A happy, secure childhood helps. Living in a properly secure environment, one learns to adventure to the limits of one's abilities without suffering consequences so adverse that one will become fearful of acting. But all that a happy, secure childhood can offer is demonstrative proof that willing need not be unpleasant. No amount of love and comfort can transform the attractiveness of the exercise of the will into the assertion of the capacity for it. Being objectively competent at various activities also helps. If one is demonstrably competent in athletics, persuasive in speech, genuine in love, skilled in intellect, that is proof positive that one could assert oneself if one would. But that is like saying that anyone could stop smoking cigarettes if only one would; in the gulf between could and would, the self is just a shadow.

Self-assertion is self-creation. One gives oneself a self-image of competence at willing by exerting the will which makes the image true. To exercise will is, by that exercise, to cause a reality to exist which was not necessitated by antecedent conditions. The brute necessity of self-assertion lies at the bottom of the question of psychic integrity.

There is no such thing as willing oneself to feel capable of willing in general. Rather, one wills oneself to *be* capable of willing specific crucial things. These have basically to do with the involvement of desires and reason in willing.

One who feels oneself to be incapable of willing believes one's actions stem from the wills of other people or from controlling conditions. Of course, consciously one might deny this. But on examination one reveals an unwillingness to do something because it contravenes the wishes of one's parents; or one's rage at feeling rejected by parents, with its attendant guilt, sets one compulsively to please one's own sense of what the parents would approve, or to please surrogate parental figures. One can claim to be engulfed by the will of others so that one does not have to be a person in one's own right; this evades responsibility.

Besides dependence on parents, one's self-image can project impotence if it presents life as caught in a deterministic causal web. One can believe that one's character, abilities, and possibilities are fixed by factors out of one's own control, such as environment, heredity, age, and station. There are some fixed factors, of course, which is what makes this kind of self-image so seductive. But one could alter one's condition somewhat if only one would, and the self-image of being determined contributes to impotence. Perhaps there is some deeper reason why one likes to see oneself as determined: that self-image sounds so much like an excuse. Whether one is brought up with such a self-image or whether one chooses it unconsciously for subterranean reasons, it must be rectified if psychic integrity is to be possible.

To correct the self-image of dependence, independence must be asserted and made part of a new self-image. Independence has the general form of distinguishing one's own desires from those of the parental figures or from the influences of controlling conditions, and of asserting them. The distinction is not in the contents of the different desires. The content may be the same in both cases. The distinction is in the ways one holds or has the desires. If one simply desires certain things as a naïve expression of one's personality or for their intrinsic attractiveness, they are one's own desires. But if one desires things which one believes one's parents to desire *because* they desire them, with fear or guilt operating as sanctions, they are not one's own desires.

The self-image of oneself as independent requires the discerning of a set or area of desires as belonging genuinely to oneself, and the conceiving of oneself as resting in those desires. One may use the assertion of that self-image, with its consequent pursuit of those desires, as the act of self-assertion by which one gives oneself an image of being competent at willing.

The environment in which one is raised and in which one lives as an adult makes a great difference to one's assertion of one's own desires and to one's self-image as a competent agent. Smothered in love or coldly rejected at the first sign of assertiveness, one has a vastly more difficult time than if one is loved by parents desiring one's own autonomy. To have one's adult roles defined in terms of subordinate positions to other people—spouse, friends, boss, society—where self-assertion is objectively punished, is also to have a more difficult time. In a sense, one's self-image as a dependent person incapable of asserting one's own will is a true image, but it is true only if one lets it be. One could change all that, at whatever the objective cost, by willing oneself a new image.

The basis of responsibility is that one *can* understand and approve the desires out of which one acts. A desire does not belong to one in a mature way until one takes responsibility for it. This is the contribution of reason to the purification of a person's self-image as free. Of course, reason is also involved in finding good reasons for approving some desires and not others, for acting here and not there; but this is not the function of reason here in question. Reason is meant here in the aspect which Kant had in mind when he spoke of practical reason. Practical reason is willing something because it is approved. Merely having a desire is one thing; a person does not have to be much of a self merely to have desires. On the other hand, to have a desire in part because it is approved by principles definitive of oneself is to take possession of that desire in a way which creates a new dimension of personality. It defines one's character as being freely constituted by the choice of those approved desires.

The notion of approving desires is vague. It can mean: (*a*) one's acknowledging that one has a certain desire and accepting oneself as the person who has it; (*b*) one's sorting among one's desires, approving some as appropriate for one's heart and others as inappropriate; or (*c*) one's sorting among the desires which one has de facto and approving certain of them as worthy of being acted upon, the others as worthy of being inhibited. The first meaning is valid for the previous discussion; one must come in touch with one's desires and accept oneself as having them. For instance, one might have to acknowledge simply that one acts as an extension of one's parents, repressing desires unique to oneself; that acceptance is a starting point for change. The second meaning is strange and not quite relevant here: one does not pick and choose one's desires and feelings as one does one's wardrobe; or as one picks overt actions. The rectification of the contents of desires, a very difficult process, is a matter of sainthood, not discipline. The third meaning is relevant here. Of all one's desires, one can choose some to act upon, rejecting or inhibiting action on the others. Those which one chooses are adopted as definitive of one's personality in their consequences. They are more oneself than the others because one has chosen them to be expressed in one's character and in the historical events which one determines.

The development of a self-image of a free agent is hardly anything special to spiritual heroism. Even those who reject any spiritual discipline beyond that demanded by mere social existence ought to take themselves to be free in the senses specified. But this kind of freedom is a necessary step upon which other kinds of spiritual development are built. One cannot exert spiritual discipline upon oneself until one *is* oneself in this minimal sense.

The order of degrees of accomplishment is not always the same as the order of time. One does not have to be perfectly self-possessed before one begins to discipline one's action, consciousness, or devotion. In fact, the problem of self-possession is raised again whenever there is a significant change in life's circumstances. Nevertheless, the degree of accomplishment at the higher levels has substance only to the extent that it is made possible by the preliminary steps. The purification of will in self-image is a peculiar step, however. For every development along the line produces an alteration in the person's self-image. In a sense, then, its purification is the last step. Yet the problems of purifying an image which includes this high accomplishment in action, consciousness, and devotion are far more complex, though far less fundamental, than those required for establishing an image of autonomy.

PURIFICATION OF WILL IN ACTION

In a general sense, action is any human movement related to desires or intentions, conscious or unconscious. In the context of the question of psychic integrity, however, action is a problem because it can be deficient in its very form. Form here is distinct both from the goal of the action, which may be good or bad, and from its content, which may be successful or not in reaching the goal and at appropriate prices. Form means, rather, the style or harmony by which the activity expresses psychic integrity. The question of form is whether or in what degree one is "present" in the activity in a rich human way. Or is one moving toward the goal with graceless incoherence? The presence of good form in action is a matter of disciplining *reason's* involvement in the action dimension of will.

Incoherencies in the form of action may take place in many areas. One may simply be physically awkward, incapable of moving gracefully and efficiently. Such grace is to some degree dependent on a felicitous nervous system and body structure; but mainly it can be learned. This is where physical education comes in.

Incoherencies are also to be found in the inner, more mental, processes of activity. One may not have learned to inhibit blind impulses well, to deliberate consistently, to appreciate motives, or to marshal various psychic and physical forces in order to make a concerted, unified move. Learning to decide and to act with a mature, strong will is a difficult process of education. It is rather like the kind of self-control learned in mastering music. These incoherencies are not so much having mistaken cognitions or unkempt appetites as having an uneducated will.

For a great many reasons, more philosophical (Descartes) and cultural (scientific thinking being construed as the pre-eminent human activity) than religious, the heritage to which most of us are socialized emphasizes a distinction between soul and body which has been disastrous to education. Physical and intellectual educations have been conceived quite apart from each other. Even when education is not formal, most Westerners have been taught that knowing things is one matter, "body building" another.

As a result, the complaint about incoherencies of form in activity perhaps most often voiced today is expressed as a disjunction between activities usually associated with mind and those associated with body. One often feels out of touch with one's body. Even in physical education one sometimes is led to feel that one's body is a mere tool rather than a basic constituent of one's self.

The outcome of the disjunction is anomie, a loss of the individual's sense of identity as a personal agent. One does not discover oneself merely in one's body and its sensations. Yet the mind conceived out of intimate connection with the body is merely universal mind, nobody's mind, not the mind of *someone*.

Freudians tend to believe that much of pathology is to be understood in terms of the obsessive's or schizophrenic's dissociation of thoughts from feelings, not of psyche (spirit, reason, and appetite together) from body. There is a great truth to this. But the dissociation of thought from feeling is dependent on a prior incapacity to invest oneself personally in the physical aspects of one's activity. To have that capacity, the psychic functions of one's thoughts, aggressive emotions, and feelings or appetites must be sufficiently integrated for one to be present to oneself in one's body. Those psychic functions may be in contradiction to each other; there may be terrible anxiety and lack of consciousness where it is most needed. But they cannot be dissociated from body if one has good form in one's activity.

How far should this general point be pushed? Do spiritual soldiers need to be athletes as well? Can there be no psychic integrity of heroic proportions for those whose bodies are halt or ill-formed? Obviously there can be! Many of the greatest spiritual heroes of history are those who triumphed over physical affliction. The point is, they engaged their physical limitations and triumphed. They engaged their bodies at the points of their disabilities and pushed themselves to the limits. A person paralyzed or blind or even just awkward may have far more invested in his or her body than one "merely normal." Of course, awkwardness may simply be inattentiveness, but that can be cured. Whatever one's physical limits, whether they be within the range of athletic excellence or not, psychic integrity demands that one reach and strain against them. The tautness of a disciplined psyche manifests itself in tautness of physical life.

The feeling of need for this tautness has manifested itself in the interest many Westerners have in various forms of breathing and posture yoga, in the ability of Zen meditation to focus and purify the senses, in exercise forms such as T'ai Chi Ch'uan and other kinds of Oriental martial arts. Even the somatically oriented forms of psychotherapy such as are practiced at Esalen, in bioenergetics, and in some kinds of encounter groups are responsive to this need, however much they ignore the complexities of much else in psychic life.

The purification of will in action is not merely a matter of integrating body and mind with good form, however. Actions take their form from the intentions or desires guiding them, and those desires need purification. The classical discussion of this is in the Bhagavad-gita. The setting is a battle between the forces of virtue and honest government, whose warrior hero is Arjuna, and those of Arjuna's cousins representing evil and corruption. As the battle is about to begin, Arjuna breaks down and cannot bring himself to act. He complains to his charioteer, the god Krishna, that no possible fruits of the battle could justify the inevitable slaughter. He must fight not only evil opponents but his friends, relatives, and teachers who serve on the evil side out of feudal loyalty. He would rather die than fight, no matter how righteous the cause.

In our own time when pacifism is a plausible moral attitude, it is crucial to see that this was not the issue in the Bhagavad-gita. Arjuna's point is not that it is immoral to kill, even in a righteous cause; the righteousness of his cause is taken to outweigh any such scruples (whether we would agree with that judgment in analysis of the dramatic action is another matter). Arjuna's point is, rather, that *he could not act* when he contemplated all the possible results of the battle. Arjuna says:

> When I see my own people arrayed and eager for fight, O Krishna, my limbs quail, my mouth goes dry, my body shakes and my hair stands on end. [The bow] Gandiva slips from my hand and my skin too is burning all over. I am not able to stand steady. My mind is reeling.[1]

Krishna then points out to Arjuna that his very problem lies in the way he contemplates the fruits of his actions. After some intellectual arguments to counter Arjuna's attempt to justify his failure to act on intellectual grounds, Krishna says:

> To action alone has thou a right and never at all to its fruit; let not the fruits of action be thy motive; neither let there be in thee any attachment to inaction. Fixed in *yoga* do thy work, O Winner of Wealth (Arjuna), abandoning attachment, with an even mind in success and failure, for evenness of mind is called *yoga*. Far inferior indeed is mere action to the discipline of intelligence, O Winner of Wealth (Arjuna), seek refuge in intelligence. Pitiful are those who seek for the fruits of their action. One who has yoked his intelligence [with the Divine] (or is established in his intelligence) casts away even here both good and evil. Therefore strive for *yoga*; *yoga* is skill in action. The wise who have united their intelligence

[with the Divine], renouncing the fruits which their action yields and freed from the bonds of birth, reach the sorrowless state.[2]

The crux of this is that the yoga of action focuses attention exclusively and completely in the action itself. Insofar as action is concerned, the external results of the action are to be put out of the mind. The only legitimate motive is to perform the action well. Perfection of the form of the action itself is the only good to which the agent has a right. The actor should be completely present in his action. No part of his effort should be distracted by ulterior motives regarding consequences either for himself or for others. He should not even think about the fact that acting well will make him a good actor. His ego has no place, only his action.

The amorality of this doctrine makes it difficult to accept. Consider the action alone. Its virtue consists, not in the causes which it serves, but only in its own form. Soldiers may embody the heroic ideal no matter which side they fight on. Our liberal fear of the soldier as mercenary, as technician, as well-oiled machine, stems from this element of amorality. The "mechanical" image is inappropriate, since soldiers whose action is personal and bodily are engaged in a very human enterprise. But our fear of the amoral hero is well-founded. (The image of the amoral person with perfect agency is not limited to the military. There are "religious" images of the perfect actors whose attention and whole being can be focused with complete intensity. Witches and warlocks are conceived as equal to the prophets and yogis when it comes to purity of action.) Purity of action is not the only ideal for actions, to be sure. Actions also ought to be moral in particular, characteristic of general moral character, and congenial to a moral society. One's cognitive abilities must come into play in deliberation, and the character of one's appetites should be perfected regarding the larger motives of action. These concerns should be attended to before any particular action is engaged. Otherwise the action, however formally perfect, will be immoral. The amorality of the yoga of action is dangerous only when it is taken by itself.

With regard to the process of spiritual development, however, there is a sense in which the yoga of action *is* to be undertaken before reason and appetite can be perfected. Ability to act with formal integrity is a rock-bottom concern which has led most spiritual traditions to risk the development of moral monsters—those tremendously effective agents with no internal morality. Why?

The answer lies in the fact that relinquishing the fruits of action requires elimination of the ego. This is a prior condition for all the higher senses of psychic integrity and moral behavior, however paradoxical it seems in connection with the need for an assertive self-image. What is meant by elimination of the ego?

One has an ego by virtue of the fact that the pattern making sense of one's actions reflects one's own career through time. The actions are meaningful not only intrinsically and in their separate contexts but also in the various senses in which they play back upon one's identity. When Krishna says that the actor practicing the yoga of action has no right to the fruits of the action, he means to deny the validity of acknowledging the ego or personal identity of the actor which takes its meaning from the fruits of the action.

This is a central tenet of spiritual realism. Any action is what it is in its own context. It accomplishes its end with a certain form. It has consequences following from it in objective fashion. Some of these consequences, of course, may be effects on the actor. But only those consequences on the actor are legitimate which are the result of objective structures of nature. What is *illusory* and to be denied are the consequences which one *superimposes* by giving the action a meaning for one's own personal identity. The reason this superimposition is illusory, and ought to be denied, is that it sullies the actions with selfish regard; one attends no longer to the clean lines of the action and its objective consequences but only to its fruits for one's own ego. In a sense, of course, to do this itself is to have objective consequences for one's ego; but they are disastrous consequences for the integrity of one's psyche. Instead of being able to put oneself fully into acting, one partially withdraws from that objective investment in the world into the imaginative construction of one's own ego. In extreme cases this leads to a plain inability to get moving, such as beset Arjuna.

Another way of making this point employs the notion of narcissism as developed by Ellis, Nacke, and Freud. As narcissistic, one sees the world primarily in terms of what it means *for oneself*; one interprets things and events primarily according to the roles which they play in enhancing or threatening one's self-image. Although one may not be blind to the objective characters which things have, one's view of the world is distorted by the narcissistic requirement somewhat to neglect things irrelevant to one's self-image, to deny or exaggerate things destructive to that image, and to overvalue the things which flatter one. While some people are narcissistic to the point of serious malady, most are narcissistic to some degree. Their actions are always encumbered to some degree by a selfish regard for the world in which they act.

A careful distinction must be drawn between one's self-image and one's ego. A self-image is a set of beliefs about how various things are available to one in one's responses to the world. Anything used in such a response— be it an emotional, cognitive, or overt response—is part of one's self. A self-image is a kind of map of how these responses are put together. For a truthful person, a self-image can be an objective delineation of who one is. The boundaries of identity shift from context to context, and this shift can be reflected in a self-image. In some contexts one can feel a grand expanse of nature or a broad sweep of history or culture as part of oneself, as the resources which one brings to a moment of response. In other contexts those things seem alien to one, and one's sense of identity sets itself off over against them. The degree of solidity of the contents of one's self-image, and the degree of permeability of the boundaries, also vary from context to context. One's sense of presenting one's public identity and withholding one's private identity varies in a crowd, with a group of colleagues, with a close friend, and with a lover. A variety of objective factors determines appropriate degrees and styles of including and bounding off factors imaged as parts of oneself. Most of us learn pragmatically who we are in different contexts. One of the factors in schizophrenia, however, is an inability to identify an appropriate self-image with its useful boundaries in certain crucial contexts. From the standpoint of the pursuit of psychic integrity, it is necessary to note that there may be a context in which it is appropriate to collect *no factors as belonging significantly to oneself*: namely, the context in which things are considered with respect to simply being what they are, not what they are *for* some other thing.

One's ego, by contrast, is a particular self-image functioning in such a way as to make one feel in possession of a certain status vis-à-vis other people. Although the components of one's identity are determined by pragmatic connections relevant to the context and to the responses made there, one's ego functions to make one believe that there is some kind of substantial self which is oneself, with accomplishments which must be magnified and deficits which must be hidden until they are made up. Instead of merely collecting the proper resources to act in a situation according to the merits of the case, with an ego one adds to one's action the considerations which will enhance the status defined by the ego. One acts not so much to do the good but to make oneself a good person. With an ego one is selfish in a literal sense of that word. Everything one does is adjectival to one's ego.

An ego is an illusion. The content of one's self is indeed relative to context and response. To allow a certain self-image to function with an absolute status defining a "self" is to live a kind of falsehood. Of course, sometimes one really does that, and in this case the ego is not illusion but lie. To have an ego which is characterized this way is to live a lie which corrupts action.

To discipline the will in experience, then, is to purify action. The corruption of action stems from the division of its directive intent between the intrinsic goal of the action and the selfish service of the ego's status. Purification of action requires the abandoning of the fruits of actions as they bear upon the ego, in effect, abandoning the ego. The only contents worthy of inclusion in one's self-image in a certain context are those determined as relevant to the objective demands of the context.

The rational purification of form in action, the spiritual purification of personal presence in the continuity of body and mind, and the appetitive purification of desires by focusing them on the intrinsic merits of the action itself constitute the aims of the discipline of action. The first is attained by the practice of discerning the essential contours and limits of an action. The second requires the practice of pure movement. The third, aided by habits of focusing intently and exclusively on actions in their formal integrity, requires learning to discriminate between desires whose objects have intrinsic merit and those which have been corrupted by the seductions of an illusory ego.

PURIFICATION OF WILL IN CONSCIOUSNESS

Consciousness is by no means the whole of experience. Civilization did not need Freud to discover this. But consciousness has two very important functions in the development of spirit, quite apart from its role in cognitive understanding and moral deliberation. First, consciousness is the primary vehicle by which attractive objects are set before one's capacity to desire. Second, consciousness renders a special focus to experience, giving it an intensity far beyond what one would expect as an ordinary outcome of a vector of natural forces; this intensity can either bind one to the flow of natural forces, or present an unusual freedom. With regard to both these functions, psychic integrity requires a kind of control over consciousness. The purification of consciousness in the aspect of desire is detachment. Its purification in the aspect of reason is the distinguishing between the objects of consciousness and the acts of consciousness. Its purification in the aspect of spirit itself is control.

Whether or not one is on a spiritual path of some sort, one recognizes that there are some objects the thought or perception of which tempts one to disaster. Some of these seductions are universal. Others, possibly the main portion, are idiosyncratic weaknesses, snares on which our proper names are stamped.

The desires excited by such objects are bad in perhaps three ways. First, the pursuit of those desires may be intrinsically evil and destructive, involving, for instance, sadistic brutalization of others, corrupting lust, necrophilic gluttony. But, second, whether or not those desires themselves are evil—and many of the worst kinds are intrinsically harmless—they are bad because they enslave the person holding them. Instead of being able to respond objectively to the values of one's life's situations, one spends too much time in the distorted pursuit of, or resistance to, those desires. In various degrees our lives are shaped, not by honest, objective response to situations, but by the blind careers of our passions. For the spiritual seeker, those desires are bad in yet a third way, for they distract from the spiritual pursuit. "Distract" is too mild a word. They undermine progress and show that the discipline attained is a will-o'-the-wisp to the degree of the distraction.

Two common responses are made to control corrupting desires. One is the rejection of all desires, severe asceticism, the renunciation of all passion, and the retreat to pure passivity. From Jainism to Jansenism, severe asceticism has been an attraction. But it is practically impossible and, where achieved in any significant degree, has often seemed more like constipation than liberation. The other response has been the embracing of all desires and pushing them to extreme expressions in the belief that they can be conquered by incorporation. The tantric tradition has been most explicit about this, but antinomianism has found its forms everywhere. The difficulty here is that hardly anyone can ride the horse to the finish without getting thrown.

Between these two extremes is the middle way, acknowledging that valid distinctions can be made between good desires and bad, and between too much and just enough. Furthermore, the content of life comes from its finite pursuits, viewed subjectively as desires and objectively as activities in pursuit of ends. The ascetic has an empty life; the erotophage, a formless one. The middle way is to find those desires and their proper objects which make finite life meaningful without corrupting it or frustrating its higher forms of development.

Determining what those proper desires are is one of the main tasks of reason. It is a matter of public as well as private responsibility, and the propriety of desires surely varies from context to context. This function of reason is not of concern here, however. The question for will, rather, is: How are the results of deliberation made effective? How is the great quiver of Eros' arrows so sorted that only those of the middle way get shot?

The answer of the spiritual traditions is that the pruning of desires requires a change in one's ordinary relation to the desires themselves. Ordinarily, the content of one's affective life *is* one's desires. The change is to introduce *detachment* from them.

Detachment is not the same as renunciation. To renounce a desire is to reject it, or to reject its object. Detachment from a desire neither accepts nor rejects but objectifies and observes it. A distinction is introduced into the psychological processes of a person between the flow of affective life and a higher level consciousness of this flow which can then select which desires to act upon according to the dictates of deliberation. With detachment, a desire is seen not with the subjective feeling of its tug but with a dispassionate observation that it is a tug. The desire is seen as a fact of attraction, and the attraction involved does not distort the clarity of the vision of it.

The roots of detachment are in all the relative and shifting inhibitions which one is taught and which one teaches oneself in daily life. One comes to be detached by setting up countervailing attractions providing deliberation and decision room within the flow of affections. But there is a difference between inhibiting the attraction of one object by balancing it against that of another (the way a baby must balance the pleasures of forbidden bodily functions with the pleasures of being loved) and inhibiting the attraction by detachment. In detachment there is the development of a psychic faculty or level of self-existence which one can inhabit without being moved by attractions singly or in balance; it is a level of life without "affection."

That such detachment is possible is an ancient observation. In the Samkhya and related schools of Indian philosophy there is a cosmology which explains it. The world consists of two things, nature (*prakriti*) and person (*purusha*). "Nature" is the unfolding and interplay of various factors, including both material and psychological elements. All the psychological functions of perception, reason, will, and desire are natural products of evolution, save pure consciousness alone. "Person" is pure consciousness, pure awareness. Psychic nature and consciousness are together in any given individual, and this itself constitutes the human problem. One confuses one's consciousness with the content of consciousness. There are no acts of consciousness which are not determined by the form of their objects and by the attractive and repulsive aspects of their affective side; but they are all natural determinations of consciousness, not the pure consciousness itself. The really real individual, according to Samkhya, is the pure consciousness which is not to be confused with the forms and affections of its objects. In learning to discriminate between the determinations of consciousness and its pure awareness, one achieves salvation by finding that one has never been bound in the first place. The feeling of bondage to entrapping desires was a mistaken confusion of pure consciousness with its objects in nature.

The cosmology here need not be taken seriously except insofar as it points out a dimension of experience. It is indeed possible to learn to discriminate between the structural and affective determinations of conscious experience and the pure sense of being aware of them. Detachment is not having a second act of consciousness observing the first, the way a second-level judgment can choose between balanced countervailing attractions. Detachment is, rather, a subjective quality of an act of consciousness itself, in which the affective elements of the act are contrasted with the elements of their being observed. This is an extremely complex form of consciousness which maximizes both passionate affect and dispassionate observation.

Although the yogic recommendation for detachment includes the closing off of the senses in the manner of a turtle withdrawing its limbs into its shell, detachment does not involve insensitivity. In fact, quite the opposite. One's ordinary narcissism distorts perceptions by having to combine the objects perceived with other factors rendering them congenial to one's ego. With detachment it is possible to perfect one's ability to see straight. Detachment is a prerequisite for connoisseurship. There is nothing a detached person has to deny or distort.

This freedom of accurate perception holds for perceiving one's own feelings as well as for perceiving "facts." With the development of detachment, the need for repression is progressively reduced. There are no affections which cannot be acknowledged for what they are through a detached sense of self. Detachment allows for a maximization of objective perception and affective experience.

On the other hand, detachment allows for a purification of awareness itself, the other side of the contrast. As long as one's acts of consciousness are dominated by affective pushes and pulls, there is much which one does not notice. With detachment, awareness of detail and discriminations of variations in importance are perfected. As it is put in Northern Ch'an

Buddhism: the mirror of consciousness is burnished until it reflects with no distortions. As it is put in Southern Ch'an Buddhism: there is not even the substance of the mirror, only the pure awareness of objects.

The heart of detachment is the holding together of both pure awareness and the experiences of which one is aware. This is quite different from the *dissociation* of thought from feeling characteristic of schizoid and schizophrenic personalities. Dissociation is not a perfection of the pure awareness of affective content, but a separation of those acts of consciousness which involve feeling from those which involve thought so that there are not even proper logical and inferential relations between feeling and thought. Dissociation involves the alienation of feeling from cognitive processes. It is a perverted form of the ordinary process of inhibiting untenable desires with other countervailing desires. According to many psychoanalysts, the countervailing desires are the obsessions with status which compensate for infantile guilt.

Spiritual soldiers with disciplined detachment are neither unemotional nor passive. But the emotions which they adopt as definitive of themselves and of the actions in which they put their disciplined activity are those approved by a higher psychic faculty than that to which they immediately appeal. The soldiers can be perfectly present in them because they put themselves into them from a state of detachment. They choose, not because of psychological coercion, but because of merits discerned from other deliberation. If the deliberation is accurate, the soldier more than any other can act according to the objective merits of the case, not according to the distortions of ego or the impulses of desires. In Freudian terms: detachment frees one from both ego and id.

The purification of will in consciousness requires the disciplining of reason as pure awareness, for the sake of detachment (this is different from other aspects of rational discipline, e.g., deliberation). With detachment and pure awareness, the spirit can then control consciousness. Control of consciousness can mean two things. First, it means that by virtue of detachment one is not coerced by desires, but can choose voluntarily among the objects of one's conscious analysis. But, second, control of consciousness means that one can select which objects of consciousness to focus on. This is a step beyond detachment. Detachment itself is practiced by meditative methods of observation and awareness. Breathing exercises, developing awareness of bodily functions, passive observation of the flow of thoughts are techniques practiced and perfected, in particular, in Buddhist spiritual traditions. Most Buddhists say that the attempt to *control* the flow of thought in this process of detachment is counterproductive. Thought must be allowed to flow in order to be observed; control introduces affective effort where there ought to be pure passive awareness. But it seems that consciousness can put its focus on objects freely if in fact it is freed from the *need* to focus on them. "Focus" is not a tool of a separate agent; it is simply consciousness modified by its object.

PURIFICATION OF WILL IN DEVOTION

Devotion is a concept greatly cheapened by religious practice. Its root meaning is wholehearted giving of oneself to an object or project with a seriousness marked by a vow. The vow lifts the devotion from an ordinary decision in the midst of relative affairs to an absolute commitment to the intention, come what may. But for many of us, devotion has come to mean the vow without the seriousness of the life lived in accordance with it. As it is used in this book, devotion is intended in its root meaning: to devote oneself is to organize all the elements of one's personality as resources to the doing or serving of some one thing.

Most of us are incapable of serious devotion. We do not know ourselves well enough to be aware of what to get together. Our wills are too weak and unsteady to subordinate all interests to the object of devotion and to keep them so arranged. We simply cannot come to the sharpness of focus required for devotion. Yet, beyond all the physical exercises, emotional disentanglements, and mental meditations, the main spiritual traditions of the world say that the way of devotion is the highest spiritual path. As Krishna says in the Bhagavad-gita, "Through devotion he comes to know Me, what My measure is and who I am in truth; then, having known Me in truth, he forthwith enters into Me."[3]

Devotion in a spiritual context has usually been taken to mean devotion to God. Yet this is a complex matter. Atheistic Buddhists are just as appreciative of devotion as are theists. This calls for a secular statement of the object of devotion before devotion can be interpreted in its spiritual context.

There is a fundamental distinction to be drawn between the regard of things as relative and the regard of them as absolute, as remarked in Chapter 1. By "thing" here is meant anything whatsoever which has an identity in any sense distinguishing it from any other thing. Among the determinate things in the world can be actual things, possible ones, conceptual, fictional or false ones, general things and particular things, positive or negative things. Any determinate thing has the character which it has by being relative to other things in differences and similarities. Its determinate character can be traced by following out its relations to its relatives. Nearly all kinds of knowledge regard things according to their relative characters, interpreting what they are in terms of their connections to other things in the world. Whatever their differences these kinds of knowledge can all be called "cosmological" because they know by relative connections within the world.

In contrast with cosmological regard stands "ontological" regard wherein things are considered with respect to their simply being what they are. Here they are considered, not as determinate with respect to this or that, but simply as determinations of being. Each thing is what it is absolutely, however true it is that its determinate character consists in relative connections with other things. Setting the boundaries of a thing is arbitrary. One may consider an electron or a state of all earth at one time. Each has the character it has because of the internal connections of its parts and the external connections with things outside the arbitrary boundaries. But each also is what it is, and no other, within the arbitrary boundary. This is the absolute nature of a thing. Absoluteness does not mean that a thing does not change or that it has its character without relative connections with other things. It does mean that within whatever time, space, or conceptual frame it is selected for regard the thing is what it is. With respect to being what it is, each thing is itself absolutely.

Devotion is the disciplining of one's life so as to enjoy the contrast of the relative and absolute aspects of the world. Regarding the relative aspect is something one ordinarily does. One must learn through spiritual discipline to regard the absolute, and then to hold them together.

An absolute regard for the world or for one of its constituents can itself be focused in two ways. The focus can be either on the determinate things considered absolutely, or on the ontological ground by virtue of which the things are. This corresponds to the theological distinction between devotion to God immanent in the world and devotion to him transcendent. Yet the transcendence of God is so unconditioned, irrelative, and empty of worldly determinations that many traditions regard the absolute transcendence as Emptiness, Nothingness, A-theos.

The purification of the will in devotion, like that in self-image, action, and consciousness, involves bringing discipline to its rational, appetitive, and spirited aspects. The spirited aspect of devotion is concentration. Concentration is the ability of the will to hold a finite object steadily in view. The borders of a finite object are always somewhat arbitrary from an absolute point of view because everything is what it is in connection with its neighbors, and each thing is equal with its neighbors in being what it is. But concentration focuses one's mind and affections on some finite object so that its definite character can be comprehended. Concentration requires the organization of one's resources into a very sharp focus of consciousness, unsullied by distractions and penumbras of feelings ordinarily associated with attentive focus.

The rational aspect of devotion is a cognitive grasp of the "what" which is the object of concentration. This kind of cognition is not so much an interpretation of the thing in terms of its causes and other connections—such cognition is cosmological and leads beyond the object of concentration—as it is an intuitive gathering together of the object's features into a pattern with integrity. It is a grasp of the "thisness" of the thing, the kind of grasp associated with aesthetic appreciation. There is a certain passive quality about the intuition, but it depends on a clarity of vision which comes from understanding and analysis. Most of all, it depends on an openness to the thing. The rational intuition of a thing's "thisness" is necessary whether the absolute is focused on as the *presence* of being in the thing or as the *transcendence* of being as the thing's ontological context. The discussion of the sage in the next chapter will spell this out in greater detail.

The appetitive aspect of devotion is the coordination of all one's desires to focus on the object of concentration. The proper desire for that object is, not to alienate it from its context, placing it within one's own nature, but rather to feel and identify with its determinate character, enjoying the values contained in that character as they are there. This is the mystic's sense of union, whose feelings and sense of things other than the object of concentration are not denied or obliterated, but so organized as not to interfere with or require the distortion of the apprehension of the object of concentration. Although this sense of union depends on a vision locating the object, it itself is a state of desire, a way of attaining to the enjoyment of an ideal value by organizing oneself in a certain way. As lover, one attains the value of the beloved by having within oneself the very form by which the beloved contains the beloved's own value. Any value the beloved is, the lover enjoys, at least to the degree of the purity of desire.

Focusing on the divine presence in the finite world, the lover attains to the value created there. Focusing on the divine transcendence in contrast to the finite world, the lover apprehends God as the creator of the value. But it is the value of the created world which is grasped in any case. Its value is grasped, not in relative terms, regarding how one thing is valuable for another, but in absolute terms, how one thing by its very form is an achievement of value. These problems will be explored more in Chapter 4.

A model often suggested for concentration is that of aiming a flashlight. Concentration is likened to the ability to control the direction of the beam and its intensity. Set in the context of devotion, the inappropriateness of this model is obvious. The problem is not to focus a projection but to organize oneself so that all one's faculties bring a certain object to consciousness in a certain way. There must be a clarity of articulation of the object, and a subjective enjoyment of it without distortion. One's consciousness must appreciate the character of the object just for what it is, considered absolutely. Spirit's task of organization for devotion is one of the highest tasks of discipline, if not the highest. It entails a self-possession sufficiently thorough and strong that one is capable of giving oneself completely to the object. No faculty or aspect of ego can stand in the way or introduce distortion. Few people, if any, attain this degree of discipline; even the greatest soldiers have cloudy vision, desires which do not reinforce the devotion, unsteadiness of will. But the ideal is a strong one.

The object of devotion must be absolute, not relative. If a thing is made the object of devotion because of its meaning or worth *for* something else, particularly for the ego of the devotee, no vision, desire, or will can be set. This is the profound truth in Tillich's famous claim that only the unconditioned can be the object of an ultimate concern. All other concerns or relative devotions lead beyond themselves to their own destruction. An object of devotion is holy if it is absolute, because, as Eliade and others have pointed out, the holy is what does not take its significant meaning from the relative connections of life.

Soldiers' devotion to duty is a model for spiritual devotion in that it aims to hold to duty even when all the relative interests of self interfere. Soldiers put their duty above all other concerns, and are so disciplined in their personalities not merely to wish their duty but to do it. So it should be with the spiritual soldier. This means, then, that the whole of the soldier's life should be organized as a life of devotion.

The life of devotion should be more, therefore, than a series of concentrated visions and loves of something absolute. It must combine a sense of the absolute with all the other attentions and intentions required for a morally sensitive life in the relative world.

Because one never is merely absolute, but occupies a relative place with particular histories, loyalties, and special duties dictated by one's station, spiritual soldiers will in all "worldly" respects seem like any other worldly people. They will be more or less fulfilled by what life brings, more or less clear and accomplished in duties, enjoying successes and suffering failures in the relative measures which are our common lot. But they will also be able to feel their place in the world as both relative and absolute. Perhaps it is the great difficulty in doing this concretely which has led most religions to provide individual personal models: Moses, Jesus, Mohammed, Krishna, Buddha, Lao-tzu, Confucius. They knew when to act in public and when to go to the hills to pray.

NOTES

1. Trans. Sarvepalli Radhakrishnan, in *A Sourcebook in Indian Philosophy*, edd. Sarvepalli Radhakrishnan and Charles A. Moore (Princeton: Princeton University Press, 1957), I.28–30.
2. Ibid., II.47–51.
3. Ibid., XVIII.55.

3

The Sage

KNOWLEDGE IS A WAY of possessing something, of taking it in. The knower appropriates the object known. A retentive mind consumes facts; what better metaphor for possession than ingestion?

Of course, to say that knowledge is possession is itself to speak metaphorically. One can know one's automobile, or one's friend, and either can still pursue an independent career. One might use one's knowledge as an instrument for controlling someone else; but the very fact that one has the knowledge and yet still needs to control means that one's possession of the object is only a manner of speaking.

Nevertheless, the metaphor of possession is not so fanciful as it seems at first. Any moment of one's experience is made up of past facts which constitute its resources. One knows one's friend by having a set of images of that friend and a discursive understanding of his or her character and intentions. Yet the basic experience out of which sophisticated knowledge arises begins in the form of direct physical feelings the content of which is past objects.

The root of the symbolic reach is the physical chain of events in the friend, the mediating environment, and one's nervous system; each member of that chain consists of the physical energy and form of its predecessor combined, according to its resources, with the other events in its past constituting its physical environment. One "possesses" the past state of one's friend as modified by the route of influence through atmosphere and body.

Important kinds of knowledge and, by consistency of metaphor, many important kinds of possession usually involve consciousness. One's physical possession of a friend is the possession only of the friend's past; the important possession would be that of his or her present and future, the kind involved in the consciousness of the friend as friend. Knowledge really involves a simplification of past facts so that the knower imagines a field with spatial and temporal depth—past, present, and future—in which known objects are projected. The structure of this basic imagination doubtless has complicated rules of construction. Some inferences can be plainly false. Yet the field of our consciousness is a field with such spatial and temporal depth, and it results from our imaginative simplification and reconstruction of past facts. We can know particular objects through time and we can have theoretical knowledge of types of objects and how they would be at any time.

The result of the possibility of knowledge—that is, of "true imagination"

—is that one in principle can be attuned to things properly, being faithful to the past, respectful of the present, and open to the future insofar as it can be known. One can comport oneself to the world according to knowledge of how it was, is, and will be; and that comportment can be attuned. Comporting oneself in the truth is not automatic, it seems. As Heidegger has argued, the most prevalent way of having knowledge is to use it to manipulate objects for parochial purposes; this causes a distortion of our knowledge of the whole. It is also possible, knowing the truth, to comport oneself deliberately in an unharmonious way. Yet those two kinds of human perversity are feeble in comparison with our simple ignorance and misunderstanding: our imagination is largely bad opinion, beset by misinterpreted perception and misplaced conventions!

Although many advances in technical knowledge have been made with the aim of controlling things, during the classical period of Greece, during the Renaissance, and in the minds of our greatest scientists of the twentieth century, the aim of knowledge has been to possess the universe in its essential points so as to appreciate its music, to vibrate to its chords. Certainly the spiritual mystic aims at communion with the universe. Where the mystical object is distinct from the world, a transcendent God, the metaphor of possession has been expressed unequivocally, except that instead of possessing, the knower is possessed. The union is perfect and transformative of ordinary finite limitations.

There is a paradox, here, comparable to that of building the self in order to lose it. The more of God and the world which one possesses, the less one is a separate possessor. To follow up the musical metaphor: one becomes yet another chord in the harmony of the whole. The subject possessing the knowledge becomes the universe. Or perhaps since the universe is the content of knowledge as well as the way by which that knowledge is ingredient in actual things, the possessor of the knowledge is God, or Pure Emptiness, the ground in which the universe is regarded as existing absolutely. The sage at the end finds that his or her knowledge as possession is empty and that the knower is not him- or herself but God, or Nothing. Buddha as the only reality is enlightenment itself.

As a spiritual model, the sage has several grades in which the rational, appetitive, and spirited parts of personality bring reason to greater excellence. The following will examine this on four levels: self-knowledge, understanding the world, becoming a person of truth, and enlightenment.

KNOW THYSELF

Like fortune cookies the oracle at Delphi often gave all-purpose advice. "Know thyself" is such an admonition. Its general applicability, however, does not make it trivial. Indeed, self-knowledge is a condition for any other kind of knowledge or activity regarding the world which requires realism.

Because any process of experience requires the integration of each item experienced with all the rest, there is an inevitable subjective bias. An item has a meaning of its own in the context in which it exists. For one to feel or to be affected by that item, to know it, or to act on it, requires one to give it a meaning within one's own experience. Its meaning derives, then, from the subjective aspects which it has by virtue of its being integrated with the rest of one's experience. When one sees a teakettle, for instance, one supplements the objective character of the kettle sitting on the stove with the subjective meaning relating it to the culture in which it is an instrument, to a like or dislike of tea, to one's attitudes toward the social function of tea drinking, to one's contingent expectations and intentions at the time. The objective meaning of the kettle must be capable of being subjectively interpreted. But the subjective interpretation may be more or less true to the kettle's objective character. The condition of the kettle's being integrated with the rest of one's experience is that some of its objective character is eliminated or compromised. But the alteration of the objective character may run between the extremes of distortion which consist in merely eliminating the trivial elements of the kettle to assigning to it a character and value which it patently does not have.

The only way one can control for the distortion one's own experience introduces into one's appreciation and intentions toward the world is to know oneself. Without self-knowledge the only means one has for detecting the nature and degree of distortion imposed on the object by its integration with the rest of one's experience is appeal to the experience of others. Although appeal to others is satisfactory in public contexts where the standard conditions of experience are well understood, it is not worth much in matters of human relationship or spiritual development. Just imagine how complex is the interplay of objective nature and subjective bias in the relation between friends, where the developing objective nature of each includes how each perceives himself or herself to be experienced subjectively by the other! Little wonder lovers worry whether their love is requited!

The first value of self-knowledge is its usefulness, even necessity, in one's self-correction of the truthfulness of one's experience. There is another value, more intrinsic to self-knowledge and in the long run more relevant to spiritual development. The immediate, intrinsic value of one's experience as such depends in part on how much of its primitive deep levels can be registered in the higher levels of consciousness. The levels beneath conscious experience include many forms of physical feeling and unconscious symbolic processes. Without self-knowledge these subterranean levels are mysteries of which one is unaware. Self-knowledge brings these levels into touch with consciousness, enriching conscious experience and making possible certain forms of integration otherwise prohibited. It should not be thought, however, that only the unconscious parts of the self are problems for self-knowledge, that the conscious elements can be taken for granted; part of our conscious life consists in the interpretation of the significance of its own contents, and that interpretation may be wrong, thus making consciousness seem other than it is.

For purposes of spiritual perfection there are three principal areas of the self into which the pursuit of self-knowledge should inquire: the rational, appetitive, and spirited parts of the soul.

Socrates introduced self-knowledge as a major theme into the Western tradition. His first and always ostensible inquiry was whether people really know what they think they know. Although there are many kinds of knowledge which we allege for ourselves and which should be assayed in self-knowledge, four are of importance for the sage.

The first is the kind of knowledge which represents itself as deriving from experience, as being filled with immediate encounter. The question to ask is whether the concrete experience is genuinely there, or whether the experience has been counterfeited by inferences as to what the experience ought to be like. There are many kinds of instances in which this may be a problem. One may think that one knows what love or anger is but in fact has never felt those emotions. Yet one can convince oneself that similar feelings or instances too weak to deserve the name show one what those emotions are. It is perhaps no moral fault that one lacks the concrete feelings; there simply may have been no occasion for them in one's experience; or perhaps one systematically prevents oneself from feeling them, which is a moral fault. But whatever, part of self-knowledge consists in determining whether one's knowledge of feelings is by direct acquaintance or by alien description.

In a more complicated vein, one may think, as a result of superficial interaction, that one knows one's friends, when in fact knowledge of one's friends would require the concrete suffering through and enjoyment of people which gives deep relationships their life-shaking power. Some people never have such relationships, and are deceived about what it is to know others.

Or again, one may think that one understands some important kind of experience, such as failure or the death of a loved one; but even if one has lived through it oneself, one may have been so dissociated from the experience as not to have appreciated its depths. Some people go through life as if they were reading it in a book.

Finally, there is the kind of firsthandedness which goes with being experienced in something. An experienced leader, craftsman, or teacher knows something firsthand from his or her experience which the novice does not, even though the novice knows the tasks, techniques, and subject matter. Of course, it is self-defeating to refrain from acting until one has the experience of it; but it is very important for one, and for those who depend on one, to understand the degree to which one has the firsthand experience.

The second kind of knowledge to assess in coming to know oneself is that in which one tells oneself one thing but knows deep down that the contrary is true. The "deep down" may be unconscious, revealing itself only in dreams; or it may be knowledge of which one is aware only in some contexts, or which is disguised in some ways, but which one denies when it would be relevant. One believes, for instance, that a certain person is a good friend and of sterling character. But deep down one knows that one is only being used in the pretended friendship and that one's friend's character is devious and manipulative. The reasons for this kind of deceit can be various. One may want to believe in the acknowledged error because it serves the ego. One may want to believe in the faithfulness of a friend in order to confirm one's own lovableness. The false belief may fit in with what one wants to believe about the world. Most citizens, for instance, want to believe that their public officials are honest and in that desire stretch the benefit of doubt beyond reasonable limits. Or one may want to believe something because the denial of it would upset the whole image of the world on which one's sanity rests; religious beliefs often reflect the sixth-grade Sunday School image of the world in which many people live.

The problem of knowing what one *really* believes, instead of what one thinks one believes, is very difficult to surmount. Perhaps it can be accomplished by reflecting in a relaxed way on the consistency of one's beliefs. Perhaps the analysis of dreams and of Freudian slips helps to uncover unconscious contradiction. But in the long run this kind of self-knowledge comes through understanding how one's emotional responses and overt actions are directed by beliefs. When one lives in existential contradictions, one's beliefs are contradictory. Of course, one may believe both sides of a contradiction because of diverse evidence; only more study resolves that, if it can be resolved at all. Usually one thinks one believes only one side.

The third kind of knowledge to inquire about concerns theory. The diverse beliefs which arise in the course of experience have implications one for the other. Yet one cannot correct them, drawing out the implications, until one has a perspective from which one can view them together, and a common language to articulate that vision. That is, one needs a theory. As Socrates pointed out, most people derive what they believe the implications of their limited knowledge to be without a theory; the result is the gross misrepresentation of what the unfamiliar experience is supposed to be. The horse-trainer's view of how to run a government is an absurdity. The first kind of test of the appropriateness of one's theoretical conceptions is whether the language in which they are couched can be generalized beyond the experiential domain in which it took its rise. One reflecting on this kind of phenomenon sometimes finds that one has no theory at all.

More often than not, however, one reflecting on the consistency of one's beliefs finds that one has two or three mutually incompatible theories operative at the same time. The shock of discovering this is far greater than that in discovering that one has no real theory to speak of. The implication of such a clash between wholesale theories is that entire areas of previously settled knowledge are called into question. Of course, if one has an investment in believing all the theories, then there is considerable pain in having to give up all but one. Yet self-knowledge requires the investigation.

The fourth kind of knowledge which must be assessed if one is to know oneself is one's image of oneself. One's self-image includes not only beliefs about one's capability as a voluntary agent (as discussed in the previous chapter), but also beliefs about what one knows and desires, about one's ancestry, status, and effects. The *result* of self-knowledge should be a true self-image. But whether it is true or false, one has a self-image which functions with respect to one's other knowledge, serving to relate that knowledge to one's enjoyments and actions. It is important to understand just what that self-image is. The difficulty with this was discussed in the previous chapter. The development of a true self-image should be the goal of self-knowledge.

Self-knowledge of what one knows is related to self-knowledge of what one desires. Knowledge of desires is more difficult to come by than knowledge of knowledge. One's desires are not formulated into words; one's knowledge, alleged or real, often is. Given the nature of desire, it can be discerned in two main ways. One can look at the pattern aimed at which, if realized, would satisfy the desire; most desires are named by their goals. The pattern is an ideal which gives structure to action by relating activities as means and ends. On the other hand, one can look at the actual strivings and urges. These are the actual factors of life which are supposed to make sense together in the light of some goal which is being pursued. Yet in fact they may not make sense that way, and the question must be put whether the desire's goal has been correctly identified. One may believe that one desires to study a certain subject; but when the time comes one always manages to get oneself distracted; the actual strivings which one had identified as a scholarly interest are really desires for something else.

Desires might be misidentified for a variety of reasons. Simple ignorance, for one; one might not know what would satisfy certain urges. Or one might have one's basic desires wrongly organized; a desire to be loved might be grouped with a desire to act competently, resulting in a sadistic goal of controlling people, for instance. One's actual strivings might point in a certain direction, but one believes that the goal in that direction is unacceptable; so one tries to direct one's strivings elsewhere, with frustration the result. The truly satisfying goals might be socially unacceptable and one fears social disapproval. Or they might go contrary to other values which one holds to. Or they might simply be repugnant on aesthetic grounds. Self-knowledge requires the analysis of actual strivings and inquiry into whether the goals pursued in their names are adequate to their satisfaction. The interest of self-knowledge is not the technical one of satisfying the desires, but the cognitive one of discovering who one is. The very content of one's life is the complex, dynamically changing set of erotic drives, guided by cognition and integrated by will. One may desire to be other than one's desires reveal one to be. Yet self-knowledge is not complete without an understanding of what one actually desires. What one really believes and what one really wants are connected with what one really wills. Will is the habit and particular capacities to integrate oneself in various ways, with effects on outer circumstances. Sometimes will is identified with desire: the character of one's will is determined by the objects one wills. This is a mistake. Will is not the desire but the way one *pursues* that desire in connection with the other things desired. Will is the ability to put one desire before another in the order of life. Which desire *ought* to have precedence is a matter for reason to determine; which desire is *believed* to deserve precedence, rightly or wrongly, is also a matter for reason. Whether the desires are genuine or counterfeit is a matter of the desires themselves. But whether they can in fact be ordered as reason says is a matter of will.

One may believe that one wants to know the truth when a lie would be more pleasant; but whether one has the will for that depends on how one inclines when given the choice. A patient with a serious disease can usually indicate to a physician whether he or she wants to know the truth, and this indication can come through clearly even when it contradicts the patient's explicit words. One may believe that one wants to follow some spiritual path, but in the crunch succumbs to the attractive temptations. One may believe that one wants to give up smoking, but if every day one has to give it up again, one's will is not what one thinks it is. Most people have fairly much the same desires, arising out of our common condition. But the differences between people which are not explained by overtly historical circumstances derive mainly from differences in will.

One of the results of self-knowledge is humility. Given the disparity between the ideals which people like to have for themselves and people's actual characters, there is a lot to be humble about. Humility is the beginning of sagacity.

Self-knowledge is a virtue in any kind of activity in personal and social life. It is not limited to the needs of putative spiritual heroes. But it has a special function in the pursuit of spiritual perfection. The aim of spiritual development is to improve the self, by stages transcending the desires, beliefs, and will of previous stages. Spiritual perfection should transform the self, killing the old and creating the new. Yet the most common temptation is to engage in spiritual activities to serve the self. Nothing flatters the ego more than something indicating that the ego is holy. Spiritual activities allow for greater personal fakery than nearly any other domain of experience. And the people most often taken in are the seekers themselves. One thinks that one wants internal improvement when in fact one wants enhancement of one's present status. More than any other dimension of experience, spiritual pursuits must be regulated by the continual effort at self-honesty. Self-knowledge in the pursuit of sagacity is not mere inquiry but the uncovering of deception. A sage is someone who at the very least knows the trickery of his heart!

UNDERSTANDING THE WORLD

Sages need to understand the world as well as themselves. But sagacity is not the same as intelligence, scientific knowledge, cultural and historical understanding, or sophisticated philosophy. The way sages need to under-

stand the world has less to do with information and theory than with understanding how all the components of public and private experience
interweave to make up the fabric of human life. Sages understand memories
and expectations, guilts and frustrations, joys and sorrows, suffering, pain,
triumph, ecstasy, nobility, depravity, honor, degradation, sincerity, men-
dacity, stress, and release. They understand the combinations and ambiguities of these in the lives of persons and in the affairs of peoples, and their
understanding allows them so to follow the trail of what is important
through the underbrush of triviality that they cleave to what is essential.

Sages are those who understand people. What people? Anyone. This is
very different from understanding themselves, although self-knowledge is
a prerequisite for a clear apprehension of anyone else. Self-knowledge also
provides many of the terms and insights leading to knowledge of others.
Yet it would seem that sages should understand people quite unlike themselves. If they are just and kind, they should be able to understand the
unjust and vicious.

Sages' understanding of the world differs from that of other kinds of
people in its intensity and degree of feeling. Although they use concepts,
and are bound to the cultural and theoretical commitments of their historical period—perhaps more so than less sage speculators—sages use concepts to *feel* with. To an unusual degree a sage grasps not only the nature
and structure of affairs in the world, but also the ways these affairs are felt
in the subjective lives of those who participate in them.

Sages' feelings need not be particularly intuitive. An intuitive feeling is
one which directly incorporates in the experiencer, with little distortion,
an isolated portion of the environment. Perhaps the best paradigm is the
aesthetic intuition of the value-character of a painting with a frame around
it. Aesthetic intuition grasps the integrity of a thing in abstraction from its
wider environment. Intuitive people are adept at empathizing with the special feelings of other persons. But the empathy extends to the feelings in
relative isolation. An intuitive person can feel the joy or grief or fear of
another person with intensity and clarity, but without feeling how those
emotions connect up with the rest of the person's life. For all their sensitivity and empathy, intuitive people are often great fools. They do not
follow out the significance of what they feel. Indeed, the clarity of intuitive
insight often precludes patience for following out the ambiguities of life.

Sages are the opposite of fools. Their feelings may lack the clarity and
intensity of empathetic intuitions, but they focus on the connections of
life, on the meanings and consequences of things. Meanings and connections are no less matters of feelings than emotions. But they are learned
from long experience, not from intuitive encounters. Sages must live
through events in order to understand their texture. By many experiences
with people they learn how human beings behave under various conditions.
Intuitions grasp things as primarily individual, particular, and unique. Sages
learn to feel the general traits of affairs. They need not think of the general
forces of existence in the abstract universals of a theory, although, of

course, they may. But they do need to have a feeling, learned usually through painful experience, for how things go. If the paradigm case of intuition is that of a work of art, the paradigm for sagacious understanding is realization of the loss of innocence. At the end of *Lord of the Flies*, when the group of castaways has sunk to mad savagery, murdered Simon, their prophet, and Piggy, their judge, and burned the island in pursuit of Ralph, the last holdout for the authority of civilization, William Golding writes:

> Ralph looked at [the rescuer] dumbly. For a moment he had a fleeting picture of the strange glamour that had once invested the beaches. But the island was scorched up like dead wood—Simon was dead—and Jack had. . . . The tears began to flow and sobs shook him. He gave himself up to them now for the first time on the island; great, shuddering spasms of grief seemed to wrench his whole body. His voice rose under the black smoke before the burning wreckage of the island; and infected by that emotion, the other little boys began to sob too. And in the middle of them with filthy body, matted hair, and unwiped nose, Ralph wept for the end of innocence, the darkness of man's heart, and the fall through the air of the true, wise friend called Piggy.[1]

Sagacity first requires that one understand people. At the heart of this is understanding how people perceive, think, and act. Most people are aware of *what* they perceive, think, and do, but usually not of the texture of their perceiving, thinking, and acting as such. These three activities constitute a person's most basic orientation toward the world. Perception is how one takes in the world; thought is how one reworks what one takes in so as to respond, and action is how one comports oneself so as to have effects on the world. Sages are sensitive to the significance of perception which is clear-cut or ambiguous, preformed by concepts or naïve, stable, conventional, kaleidoscopic, or swarming. They know the difference between imitative and reflective thought, between memory and creative reason, between abstract thinking and the pondering of concrete experience. They understand the consequences of action tentative or decisive, brief or continuous, aimed at a single effect or at a sea-change. Most people perceive, think, and act in all these ways at various times, and sages learn from experience the meaning of each in its place.

Most of the time one makes sense of things in experience by seeing how they relate to intentions. That is, one views human affairs as ordered to various interrelated and often conflicting ends. But one constantly fails to pursue one's intentions, doing things contrary to what would bring about the desired results. This is irrational behavior, and one looks to blame it on ignorance, ill-will, or mental pathology. To sage experience, however, there is a deeper kind of rationality. Sages learn from experience the general habits people have of succumbing to the spell of base temptations, of deceiving themselves about the most important things, of being too soft and lazy to develop courage in the face of opposition. Most of all, they are sensitive to these corruptions in the most excellent souls. There is no iron law of human perversity, but a sage knows when you have to count on heroism and how trustworthy that faith is.

Besides knowing people as individuals, sages understand certain universal factors in human existence which affect people individually and as groups. Perhaps the most important of these are order and chaos, freedom and necessity, good and evil, endurance and transience. Whereas philosophers attempt to understand these in terms of categories, sages understand them in terms of their various bearings on life. From experience they come to feel how these factors give human shape and meaning to life. These things and others are significant because they make life human. Of course, they always have very particular manifestations in the lives of individuals; but the humanity of those individuals is formed by the general meaning of those themes for them, not their particular clothing alone. Only by coming to understand how these themes penetrate experience are sages able to discern what is essential.

Because they understand people and the basic traits of existence, sages should be able to understand historical events. They should know the significance of the events of their own time, not trapped by parochial interests but able to grasp life as a drama. It might be thought, of course, that this is simply to say that the sage is an historian. The difference between the sage and the historian is that the former excels in feeling meanings thoroughly, the latter in discovering and interpreting evidence ordinarily obscure. A sage may know nothing about reading documents or judging sources. But there is an essential affinity between the kind of understanding which a sage has of the world and the form of understanding which guides the historian's technical craft: both take the form of drama. Human meaning is dramatic.

The terms of sagacious understanding are always relative to historical context. And, of course, it helps for sages to be aware of the limitations of historical understanding in as sophisticated a way as possible. They should understand the methodological commitments and experimental foundations of their scientific concepts. They should have philosophical rigor in the use of general concepts. And they should have their horizons expanded and purified by the professional evidence of the historian's craft. But the essential focus which sages maintain even at the cost of these professional excellences is concrete feelings. For they must be able not only to say *what* the meaning of something is but also to feel its importance. That is, sages feel the worth in something and know what its worth is for something else. No science, philosophy, or investigative storytelling craft can substitute for a direct, cumulative experience of the worth of the important themes of human life.

BECOMING TRUE

The cognitive aspect of spiritual development can be approached in terms of the objects known. The discussions of self-knowledge and of the understanding of the world have worked this way. More directly important for the personal quality of sagacity, however, are one's preparation to receive knowledge, and the effect on one when the knowledge is properly received. The more adequate one is to one's knowledge, the more one can be said to live in the truth.

Most philosophers today would say that only propositions are true; "people" are not true except when they are metaphorically identified with their beliefs. A few philosophers would say that a thing, even a person, can be called true when it conforms in an unusual degree to a relevant ideal, as when a politician is called a "true statesman." But there is a special sense in which a person can be said to be true, to live in the truth, when he or she holds knowledge in a way which keeps it pure and makes it as effective as it can be in life.

Philosophers, of course, are very clever at generalizing the concept of "proposition" to mean any fact, any definite state of affairs with a nature which can be asserted in a symbolic sentence of some sort. In this sense there would be propositions at the root level of experience whenever one abstracts characters from one's brute physical feelings and compounds them to form possible patterns for one's self-integration. A true proposition of this sort would be one in which the character compounded is *referred* to something and indeed is to be found in the thing referred to. The simplest example would be a perceptual proposition where the pattern is derived directly from a physical feeling of the object referred to. These rudimentary propositions are not as important for the present discussion as those whose components are the symbols of our socially defined world.

The reason truth is a problem, however, is easily illustrated at the rudimentary level. A proposition is true if it conforms to its object. But it is valuable in the experiencer who entertains it if it leads him or her to successful and rich integration. Put more prosaically: a proposition is true if it says of its object what the object is, but it is valuable if believing it makes the believer happy. The problem of egoism arises at the heart of believing. A rough pragmatism sets limits to the egoism of belief: a false belief acted upon may lead to disaster. But pragmatism alone does not articulate the ideal of being true when it hurts.

Because any proposition believed—or entertained in any mode, such as disbelief or suspended judgment—must be integrated with all the other aspects of one's contemporary experience, and because the interests directly guiding the integration need have no correlation with the proposition's truth (except in the roughest pragmatic way), truth is an existential problem. For one to comport oneself so as to preserve the proposition as true, not denying or distorting it, is for one to adopt the ideal for holding to the truth over and above that of attaining an integrated harmony. If one does act so as to preserve the truth, one's whole constitution, which partly takes its form from accommodating that truth, can be called true. To be true, or to live in the truth, is to form oneself so as to accommodate true propositions. Of course, one is true only in respect to the true propositions which one accommodates. It becomes *relevant* to call one true when one is true to important things, and not just once but generally.

But why should one be true when the propositions with respect to which one is true have no particular pragmatic value, and perhaps are painful? The obvious and age-old answer is that a human being living in the truth is simply better than one who disregards the truth or who lives lies. This is to say, the ideals defining human kinds of harmony are richer, and describe greater value, when they include being true over and above more immediate kinds of integration. It is similar to the difference love makes to sex; without love sexual relations provide immediate pleasure and release of tensions, and they help to maintain the population. For most species this is probably all there is to sex and the best they can do. For people, however, sex is good but love with sex is better, even when it introduces heartaches unknown to brutes (human and otherwise). So with knowledge: pragmatic accommodation to the environment is good but truth with accommodation is better. It simply is richer. And it is just one of those elements of richness which gives human life its special edge. Truth, like most things especially human, is bittersweet.

The conflict with egoism is the heart of the matter. Disregarding the special concern of being true, one can selfishly restrict the components which require integration in one's makeup. One can aim at patterns of harmony which exclude the things which it would be difficult to include. One can define oneself as being satisfied in a narrow way. Indeed, as soon as one forms a sense of ego one can say that the only values to be preserved and enhanced in one's integration are those which play roles in one's ego. Acting to satisfy one's ego is not an original, natural, or primitive orientation. By nature one simply acts to integrate the components given to one's experience, whether or not they are organized around one's ego; organizing one's actions to respect only (or mainly) the values of one's ego is a special and constricting development. But it commonly happens.

To live in the truth, or to face the problem of truth, is to confront egoism directly. To be in the truth is to accommodate the object known and the value preserved in the appreciative knowledge of it. Although that value must be *compatible* with the other things in one's experience in order to be integrated, it need not be a value which either enhances one's ego or fits well with one's special interests. The price of respecting the known object for what it is, for being true to it, may well be a frustration of one's egoistic self or personal interests.

To live in the truth is to have a kind of natural piety. Openness to a thing requires a prejudgmental reverence for it, allowing it to be and to register in one's experience pretty much on its own terms. Of course, if a thing is evil, *after* piety one should take steps against it. But not to be true to the object first would mean that even its evil cannot be judged accurately, but only according to the relatively parochial requirements of one's ego or special interests. Natural piety is a prerequisite for fully objective morality.

By adding natural piety to the respect ordinarily accorded one's personal interests for pragmatic reasons, it is possible to attend to properly general ideals. Everyone knows abstractly that a properly general ideal is one measuring what is best for all the things in view. The actual development of natural piety brings this general moral principle some concreteness. Of course, natural piety itself is an ideal component of the human norm of being true, and as an ideal it is rarely realized to any great extent. The best most of us can do is to cultivate an experience or two of awed respect for a thing apart from our parochial interests. Afterward we quickly lose faithfulness to the integrity of the respectful vision. Remaining faithful to the truth is even harder than the vision itself. The spiritual heroism of the sage is in the continued effort, returning to the lists after repeated failure.

Openness to the truth is not effected by an heroic act of will but by the slow development and reformation of one's character. There are three principal areas in which natural piety must be cultivated: resting in the truth about the world, resting in the truth about oneself, and resting in the truth of things considered absolutely, the truth about the divine presence. The borderline between things in the world and things in oneself is highly ambiguous; some things—one's body or one's past deeds, for instance—are clearly in both. The difference for being in the truth, however, is that some of the things which must be truly apprehended as being in the world may then be distorted in the context of their also being apprehended as being definitive of oneself.

Openness to things in the world means letting them come across. As Jaspers and Heidegger have pointed out, one usually addresses things in terms of their readiness to play roles in the world of human interests. One apprehends things by means of categories derivative from the pursuit of human interests. Even one's senses are cultivated to select among the possible stimuli those which bear upon one's interests. Being true to things requires letting them set the terms in which they are apprehended, supplanting those derivative from one's interests.

But, of course, it is the nature of human apperception to perceive the world through the limitations of the nervous system and to grasp it in concepts. The very limitations of the nervous system are what allow one to include as much information as one does within one's responses. Only through general concepts is one able to relate things consciously to other things, including those things necessary for apprehending them within one's own experience. Truthfulness therefore requires reworking one's senses and interpretative responses so that their contours are determined by the interest of how sensitively one's cognitive apparatus can respond to the diverse things of the world, not by one's personal interests. Having expanded personal interests to include the general interest of being truthful to the world, one must find the means of pursuing that larger interest!

Clearly, the first step is learning to pay attention. Most of the time one attends to things in the world only insofar as they present themselves as obstacles or means to the pursuit of one's interests. Certainly one cannot do without this kind of attention. Attending to the world for its own sake means at least four things. First, it means bracketing out some portion of the world for a good look! If one explicitly sets aside all pragmatic concerns and preconceptions, how does the thing reveal itself? Intuitions on the aesthetic model are of use here. Second, it means cultivating the attitude of observer on one's own experience. It is one thing to learn from experience as a participant. It is another to stand back and ask what exactly that experience is in which one is a participant; the conclusions one would draw as observer may be very different from those one would draw as participant. Both intuition and observation require much waiting.

Third, attending to the world means developing a theoretical curiosity about it. That is, how may the world, or some dimension of it, be conceived as a totality? One's usual theoretical commitments reflect the standpoint of one's personal interests, and this must be set aside in favor of a theoretical view the norm of which is true seeing, not necessarily useful seeing. This is not to say that theory is non-historical. The best and most truthful theories always reflect the development of thought at a particular time, and change with the discovery of new evidence, the invention of new research methods, and the idiosyncracies of particular investigators. But they need not be biased by narrow human interests. Fourth, proper attention must focus on the very problem of attending to the object both within and without the sphere of narrow human interests. Only in this way can it regulate the accuracy of attention itself.

The second step to natural piety about the world is to correct the senses. Various forms of sensitivity training have been popularized in recent years, derivative from Western psychology as well as Eastern yogic traditions. This is perhaps the most technological step in the process of openness, and may be left to the technological approach. Nevertheless, a continual vigilance is required to determine that the sensitivity being developed is not itself a special kind of selectivity for useful information. Some forms of behavior modification, for instance, teach sensitivity to the feelings of authority figures for the purpose of controlling the authorities; this doubtless biases the view of those feelings.

The third step is to correct the biases in one's concepts. There is a difference between saying, as we must, that all concepts take meaning through social interaction—a thing is symbolically meaningful if it is conceived to play a role in someone else's experience—and saying that the purpose of interaction is the pursuit of some narrow human interest. Some human interaction may be for the sake of getting the truth about the world! Poetry is in part an attempt to use language to get at the truth of things, breaking out of the more narrowly pragmatic sense of language. The problem is that for reasons of survival if nothing else, people *must* develop conceptions which are narrowly useful to their persons. Truthfulness requires knowing how this usefulness is a bias and inventing altered concepts to express things more directly.

Truthfulness about that part of the world which is also oneself is more difficult. All the problems discussed above concerning attention, accurate perception, and adequate conceptualization arise here. But there is the added factor that the act of registering such knowledge is a determination of the makeup of the self in light of knowledge about what the self is. *Any* registering of knowledge is a determination of the self as truthful in that regard. But when the regard is one's very self, the registering of the knowledge requires some affective adjustment. One cannot take into oneself the knowledge that one has a secret hatred of one's parents without making some response to that. The response need not be a wholesale change of character, or even a willing of oneself to "accept" the fact about oneself. But it does need to be a response identifying oneself as the knower who knows that fact about oneself.

As with purification of the will, the task for truthfulness about oneself is the elimination of the ego. For ego is the illusion about one's identity which makes one distort the truth about oneself and believe conceits in order to maintain status. Of course, one is responsible for various factors about oneself in ways in which one is not responsible for things external to oneself. But does this mean that one must identify with a status which must be maintained?

The obvious answer is no if the ego is an illusion. But the question is deeper than it seems. If one were only an actual thing, or set of facts, one's nature could be known factually. The bad truths about oneself could be accepted as misfortunes or bad choices about which something should be done. But one is not only one's actual nature but also one's ideal nature. That is, one's identity is the dynamic relation between the ideal relevant to what one actually is and one's actual accomplishments and strivings. One quite properly feels oneself obligated, and that is not a fact like other facts; it is not the result of a process but of a norm governing a process. The appeal of an ego is that it provides an answer to the concretely felt question: "What ought I to be and how close am I to it?" The ego is a conception of the self which functions as a norm for relating factors in one's experience; it provides direction for what can be accepted and what rejected, what elevated in importance, what depressed.

But an ego is a false norm, a destructive short cut. A true norm is one whose pattern measures out the best for all the components it combines. Some of these are aspects of one's self; others are not. The norms for a truthful person (whether or not he or she heeds them) are measures of benevolence toward all the things known. An egoistic person believes that, because the norms bind the responsibilities of all the components of his or her self, the norm should be a pattern for that self. Egos differ in elegance of conceptions. Some people's egos are mean, nasty, and rarely sensible beyond lust. Others' are models of elevated virtue. But the egoist who acts for the sake of his or her own virtue, rather than for the benefit of those affected, is all the more dangerous. The self-deceits and blindness of the narcissism of the person whose ego is the Great Soul cannot be topped.

Knowing the truth about oneself means responding to how well one measures up to the relevant norms. One cannot be open to the truth about what one is until one has discovered what one ought to be in remaining open to the development of that norm, in noting as well what one has in fact become. It is difficult indeed to maintain natural piety about the connection between these two.

Knowing the truth about the absolute nature of things is not "natural" but "holy" piety. In a sense, even natural piety is an openness to the absolute nature of things. It aims to know things just as they are in explicit disconnection from the biased interests of the knower. But it is one thing—natural piety—to focus on things as they are. It is another—holy piety—to focus on things in the respect that they simply exist. In knowing individuals, for instance, natural piety opens itself to "this x," "this y"; holy piety focuses on "x as a this," "y as a this." It is not a metaphysical contemplation of individuality or thisness. Rather, it is an observance of each thing as a contingent, finite entity.

Anything which exists has a nature which is ontologically contingent. If it is an actual entity existing in space and time, it is a complex individual made up of parts derivative from its past. Those parts and the limitations which they bear are the cosmological causes of the entity, in the sense that antecedents cause consequents. But that there is such a process of cosmological causation at all is ontologically contingent. The mark of the finiteness of an existing thing is its unity in complexity; even if necessitated by antecedent causes in a cosmological sense, its existence as being what has been or can be cosmologically caused is ontologically contingent on there being a cosmological process.

To know the world in its contingency is to feel the contrast between the absurd fact that it exists and the absurd fact that it need not. This might be theologically conceptualized in terms of a theory of the world's being created by a God, or by a theory of the unreality of the realm of definite things, dharmas. Whatever, living in the truth of this is holy piety in all traditions.

ENLIGHTENMENT

Beyond what sages know and are, regarding themselves and their world, there is the knowledge they have of ultimate things. This is their understanding of the truth whose possibility is holy piety.

At this point the discussion becomes controversial in a special way. No self-respecting representative of any world civilization can be against self-knowledge, understanding of the subtle ways of the world, or living in the truth, however much he may disagree with some of the interpretation given. But people may well maintain that enlightenment is illusion and its pursuit indulgence. Just as anti-spiritual people may object to the role suggested for devotion in the disciplining of will, so they may object to moving beyond the obvious contributions to psychic integrity of self-knowledge, understanding of the world, and truthfulness. Enlightenment is an experience, and those who do not have the experience simply do not have the forceful conviction which experience provides. They may read about it and accept it as a valid phenomenon because of its pervasiveness throughout different spiritual traditions. But if they are suspicious of claims about enlightenment as wishful thinking, its very ubiquity may count against it.

Nothing much can be done about this. It is similar to the case of those who are unloving and unloved: to them the claims of lovers are fatuous, if not offensive, and the language of love is even sillier than that of mysticism. The best presentation which can be made is to show how enlightenment is theoretically possible at least, desirable, and witnessed to in diverse forms.

The quest for enlightenment in the spiritual context is the search for the meaning of life. Seekers want to know why we are here. But the difficulty in the quest is not in discovering the answer; anything so basic as the meaning of life must surely leave its marks throughout all experience. The difficulty is in the question itself: What is "the meaning of life"?

The reason people in all ages and all places have asked that question seems to be that frustration always has the last word. One lives one's life with purposes, but in the end one's important intentions are unfulfilled. Things do not work out. The world does not provide one with needed luck. One gets sick and cannot go on. One gets old before one finishes. One dies. As the Buddha said, all life is filled with suffering. Even when narcotics blunt the edge of pain, not to be fulfilled is to suffer. In our own time the frustration seems so great that few even begin with the purposes which would make a life meaningful if they could be fulfilled. Life adds up to nothing.

But notice the ground from which the metaphor of life's meaningfulness arises. The prime analogate of human meaningfulness is a social role. A king is meaningful in his ruling, a farmer in his providing, a mother in her nurturing. But these are all social roles and do not provide meaning for life even if they are successfully pursued. A human life contains much more than can be given meaning by social roles. Nevertheless, the conception of life as a role instrumental to something else has been a tempting, if silly, suggestion: the meaning of life is supposed to be to win immortality (why infinitely more of the same is an advance upon a short span of intrinsically meaningless existence is an unanswered question), or to get to heaven (where there are no frustrations), to the Pure Land, to win everlasting fame, or to become superman. The problem with all of these is that the meaning of life cannot be found in something other than life itself. Heavenly life may be preferable to the earthly sort, but that is an abstract consideration and not to the point of the question of life's own meaning.

If the meaning of life is not something else toward which life itself can be a means, what is it? The spiritual traditions answer, "There is no meaning to life." That is, when life is required to have its fulfillment in something else, when it has to add up to something other than its finite round, it is simply absurd. "All is vanity," cries the preacher. "Empty," says the Buddhist. "Being returns to non-being, the ultimate result," says the Taoist. Jesus said, "The kingdom of heaven is at hand; I have overcome the world!" "Then why are you on the cross?" asked the people; "everything is the same as before!" If the meaning of life is moving from this life to a better order, heavenly or historical, life has no meaning.

The beginning of enlightenment is the recognition that the ontological character of things as simply being themselves is more important in a spiritual sense than all the meanings given by their cosmological characters. Our lives have real significance in the roles we play with respect to other people, but these are partial for us and we are replaceable in them. There are real moral obligations, personal duties to family and community, and world historical tasks. These give ideal direction to life, with some accomplishment; but when the meaning is in the final accomplishment, all is vanity. Our parts on life's stage are meaningful only relatively, not absolutely. Nevertheless, we are what we are, however fragmentary that is. Our intentions are ambiguous, usually fall short of expectation, are not what they seem when realized, and always in the long run turn to dust: but that is exactly what we are. Each of us is different in being only what he or she is. Life's meaning must be in our thisness.

The Buddhists have an elaborate metaphysical view of these matters aimed at showing that the connections required for life to add up in an instrumental way are illusions. Causation is not real in the relevant sense. Without accepting the metaphysical interpretation of causation, we can accept that a thing's being is more basic to its existence than its causes and effects. Buddhism says any thing in life is empty; that is, it has no substantiality beyond the nature which appears—it simply is. It is not caused by a more substantial cause, or by itself, nor does it exist in its effects. It is when it is and what it is.

But how does the thisness of things answer the question of the meaning of life? In the recognition that life has no meaning, radical shift of consciousness takes place: Zen's sudden enlightenment. The egoistic question "What would fulfill me?" gives way to the question "What is there to be fulfilled?" But the answer is "The things which are." The enlightened response is then attentive wonder at the "thises" of the world, a holy piety.

If there is no instrumental meaning to life, the question of meaning in the instrumental sense loses its importance. The question of meaning is replaced by the question "What is real?"

But the reality of contingent things—as all finite things are—is contingent! On what? Surely not on some primal finite thing, for that would in turn be contingent. On a primal infinite thing (God is often called an infinite being)? But if it is really infinite in itself, it is not definite, and therefore could not be the creator of this world (our creator surely is definite in that God is a this-worldly creator rather than the creator of some alternative). About the cause of the world as such nothing definite can be said, apart from what is definite about the appearance of this world. The cause is neither finite nor infinite, existent or non-existent, one or many, or any other categorial thing. In recognition of this, the ontological cause can be called Absolutely Empty as well as Pure Act, Nothingness as well as Fullness, Brahman without Qualities as well as Brahman with Qualities. The cognitive feeling and emotional realization of this contingency of the world upon an absolute ground which itself can be no thing can be described as atheism as well as theism. Yet given the history of the concept of God in all traditions of India, China, and the West which divests the deity of all finite qualities, the absolute ground can be called God without commitment to a narrow theism. Chapter 5 will discuss the question of God more directly.

If the ground in itself is Nothing, still the world is here. The ground is the Nothing out of which this world has arisen. Of course, there is no worldly seed in God apart from creation out of which the world grows—that would be to require God in himself to have a definite nature (which would itself be contingent, etc.). So the metaphor of the world arising from an absolute ground cannot be taken in a cosmological sense: a cosmic ground (but not the divine) contains seeds producing plants. Perhaps the world should be said to arise out of the Abyss, out of Chaos. But the absolute cannot be a place—spatiality is definite and therefore contingent; so the Abyss is a limited metaphor (so is Emptiness for the same reason). Chaos in its turn connotes a swarm of finite things in disorder; but if the disorder is complete, there is not even a swarm of numerically distinct things. God simply cannot be named, because anything which can be named is a contingent created product.

Should we say that the world is simply spontaneous? Of course, from the standpoint of looking for an earlier cause within the cosmic process, some things may indeed be spontaneous. But since time itself is definite and contingent, it along with all the other basic elements in the cosmic process came to be out of no antecedent time, even should the physicists put a date on a first movement. To say that the world is spontaneous is simply to repeat that it is contingent as a whole in its own terms.

What we can say is that the world is created by God. Creation here means that something definite comes to be. It does not come to be out of antecedent material, as is the rule with causation within the cosmos. There is simply an act of creation in which that for which there is no antecedent reason comes to be. The act has absolutely no character of its own except that derivative from the created product. It follows no rules or antecedent structures. Its product, the world, may embody rules, but they are as contingent as the product of which they are measures. Whitehead called the act of creation the Primal Created Fact.

But now God does have a character in a way. As the creator of this world, God has the character of being creator of this much order, this much chaos, this much necessity, this much freedom, this much goodness, this much evil. God is the creator of the world with this one's history. Discovering God's character ultimately means examining the basic traits of this world; so theology is empirical in the broadest sense.

The history of religions reveals great ingenuity on the part of various peoples in summing up their readings of God's character. Some have thought the world to be similar to what a person would produce; Judaism and Islam have reinforced personal elements in primitive anthropomorphic conceptions even as they have elevated the conceptions to ontological clarity. Christianity's trinitarian theory and Buddhism's conception of the three Buddha-bodies have seriously modified monotheistic conceptions of God as a person while retaining a strong theme of divine agency. Hinduism, Taoism, and Confucianism have stressed metaphors of emptiness and manifestation, although there is a strong personalist strain in some forms of Hinduism, such as Ramanuja's. Clearly, different aspects of creation are better represented in different theories. Even polytheism has its day in making out the diversity of things created.

From the standpoint of enlightenment, however, the theoretical conceptions are less important than a grasp of the contingency of the world, of the transcendence of its ground from any finite character, and of the presence of the creator in the world insofar as the world is the divine character. These are not three separate points, but one. Although it is a logically complex conception, from which any one part can be inferred from the others, the grasp of the conception is unitary.

But is enlightenment merely the grasp of a conception, a theory? No and yes. The theory is a concept by which the world is interpreted. Understanding the concept of the world as created and God as creator—two expressions of the same concept—a sage interprets every aspect of his or her world as divinely grounded. That is, a sage directly experiences the world that way, just as a person with the visual concept of redness can directly experience red things, or as a lover can experience the beloved's love. The conception is instrumental to direct experience. On the other hand, the cognitive grasp of the concept is the realization of something basic to intelligibility itself. As Anselm and other defenders of the ontological argument have pointed out, the experience of a certain necessity of thought reveals something directly about existence as well as legitimates an inference.

Experientially, the experience of enlightenment contains a high degree of self-certainty and authenticity. The experience seems much more direct and conclusive than sensible experiences of colors or interactive experiences of people's character. From the standpoint of theoretical claims, on the other hand, the experience of enlightenment must be asserted to be valid and assertions of that sort are always fallible. It may be true to say that the proposition "God is creator of the world" is certain. It is quite another thing to say "It is certain that God is creator of the world." The latter proposition may be true, but it cannot be certain because of the fallibility of judgments about experience. Therefore it is better to say (when speaking from a theoretical standpoint) that "Divine creation is experienced as certain." The sage need not engage very far in theoretical concerns.

The sages' grasp of finite contingency, divine transcendence, and divine presence is fruitful for their enlightened grasp of the world. In the first place, all things in the world are equal in the respect that each is created to have the nature it has. Appreciating things in their thisness, sages see that each thing is as close to God, its ground, as any other thing is. From the standpoint of cosmological differences, of course, some things are far more valuable and important than others. From the ontological standpoint, however, each thing enjoys its own being as a gift from God. If one could speak of a divine attitude, it would be the same for all creatures. God sends his rain upon the just and the unjust. Theologically, this has been known as "divine indifference."

For sages, it means they may practice a similar "indifference." Whereas in ordinary affairs, even if one is a sage, one must distinguish between things close to one and those far away, between things relevant to one's life and things not, between things good for one's own experience and things without value for one (regardless of their own values), in one's spiritual attitude one should feel equal closeness with all things. Practically, this is impossible, since one cannot even think of all things. But when two things are presented, one knows that insofar as one is relating to them as contingent creatures, they are equal and one is as close to one as to the other.

This is another blow to egoistic narcissism. Egoists make their own perspective on the world the norm for determining the importance of things. Enlightened sages know that elements of their own personality are simply among the creatures of the world and have no claim on anything else. Ontologically, things simply are; for them to be ordered as components of somebody's world is a convenient cosmological fiction. Sages do not deny that they have a limited finite nature with a definite perspective on the world. But they do deny that this definite perspective has any ontological significance beyond being what they simply are. They are as close to their neighbor's perspective as to their own. Ontologically there is no perspective for the creator; God is immediately present in each thing, with nothing in between.

If all things are ontologically equal, how are sages to act? They certainly cannot act on the principle of advancing their own finite perspective. They cannot regard their own person as any more important or worthy of consideration than anything else in experience. The only possible reason for acting in one way rather than in another, then, is the objective merit of the alternative. Sages should determine on the basis of cosmological considerations what things ought to be done and then do them. Of course, that one is a sage does not mean that one is skilled enough in deliberation to know what to do in a particular case; and even if one knows what to do, there is no guarantee that one will do what one knows one ought. But insofar as one is true to one's knowledge of divine indifference, one may not allow any considerations but objective merits to rationalize one's actions.

The enlightened sage's grasp of the connection between God and the world is also fruitful for an understanding of the authorship of activities in the process of events. Every process can be conceived as having two kinds of authors. On the one hand, there are the cosmological agents defined within the process itself: the people taking part in the events, the causal agency of living and inanimate things. Causal agency here is defined as the conditioning of later events by earlier ones. On the other hand, any process is created by God, no matter where its borders are set. God may therefore be said to be its author, though this may not be taken to imply finite divine existence. That God creates the whole process does not mean that early events within the process fail to condition later ones. There are two different senses of causation involved, cosmological and ontological. There are likewise two different senses of responsibility. Chapter 5 will be devoted to sorting these out with respect to the moral responsibility of people within the process: How can people be free when God creates them and their world in all respects?

A consequence of the double authorship of events is that every act can be viewed as God's act or as an absolute act. That is, every act is a contingent act of existing, as well as an act doing this or that. Insofar as absolute existence is holy, God's holiness can be perceived in all existential acts. As the Upanishadic tradition puts it, This is Brahm, That is Brahm. There is nothing which is not God creating.

Furthermore, because all definite things are interconnected, being defined in terms of each other, the separations between them are arbitrary cuts. There is only one act, the act of this world's existence, the Primal Created Fact, the one divine act of creation. Without blurring definite distinctions, sages can see their own reality—God acting—in all other acts of existence. That art thou. That am I.

A final aspect of the enlightenment vision is its secularity. There is no transcendent meaning to life. Life's meaning is to be God's creature, and that one already is. Realization of this is not a transportation to another world but a Zen master's lesson that the world we have is it. As the Mahāyāna Buddhists say, Nirvāṇa is Saṁsāra. The kingdom of heaven is at hand; I have overcome the world (and it looks no different). The triumph over the suffering of the usual world is the appreciation of the divine presence in it, of its ontological emptiness and dependency.

Sages, therefore, look no different from ordinary people caught in the round of Saṁsāra, except that they perhaps spend a little more time thinking. They have no aura of holiness as if from another world, and those who do should be suspected of fraud.

Yet perhaps more than others sages are devoted to the world. Where there is injustice, it should be stamped out now by those who are around; it will not be recompensed in some other domain and cannot be left for other-worldly divine intervention—those who are here now are God-present-in-history. Where there is suffering, it should be alleviated with sympathy and correction; there is no one besides us to do the task. Where there is *any* human emotion—happy or grievous—it should be entered into as the way of participating in God's world. Judgment may require entering an emotion in the form of altering it—participation does not mean approval in a cosmological sense. (Participation does mean that ontologically sages approve evil as something created in the world to be suffered and fought.) The point is, enlightenment commits one to greater participation in the world, not withdrawal or renunciation.

In conclusion, enlightenment requires the development of bifocal vision. Out of the lower focus, sagacity envisions the world cosmologically (as Saṁsāra). Here one sees causal connections, relative values, moral demands and prescriptions, and the limitations of one's finite perspective. Here the meaning of things is what they add up to, the values they finitely enjoy. Out of the upper focus (as Nirvāṇa), one envisions the world as the product of God, or Empty, contingent upon existence deriving from outside its own round, and exhibiting the presence of the creator in all its parts. Here there are no differences in perspective, nothing adds up to more than it simply is, and the meaning of life is simply to enjoy being created, with all the suffering and limited joys creation contains. These two focuses must be kept together. The lower lens without the upper represents life as absurd and encourages the indefinite postponement of responsibility in fictional hope of a *deus ex machina*. The upper lens without the lower is simply impossible; to see divine creation without the created world is nonsense; God is grasped only as creator of this world, apart from which he has no character; this is the world which is the divine Emptiness. To envision God's creation *only* under the aspect of its being created, ignoring the cosmological relations and moral obligations, is simply not to see *what* the creation is. Sages, therefore, are most secular people, participating in the contingencies of life to the fullest. Yet insofar as all acts are God's their participation is still another divine act. The more they possess the world in knowledge, the more they know it to be not particularly theirs but a divine possession. That the knowledge is from their own finite perspective is a mere contingency.

NOTE

1. (New York: Capricorn, 1959), pp. 186ff.

4

The Saint

WHICH IS BEST? To have a good will, a profound understanding, or a pure heart? To the extent that any one heroic trait can be perfected without the others, it is a mixed blessing. Without knowledge and worthy passions soldiers may be as effective in evil as in good. Without strength of will sages are ineffective, and without desires consonant with what they know to be the good they are subject to that tragic pride in their own virtue by which the wise so often fall. For all their perfected impulses, saints without toughness and thorough understanding are saps.

Despite the clear desirability of being a soldier, sage, and saint together, the focus of development in each is different. Yet within limits, there is a certain order of the focal points. Soldiers can discipline their will, even in the spiritual sense, without much firsthand knowledge of relevant things and with little reformation of desires. They can handle desires with repression; their beliefs can be conventional myths and their orders can come from others. The pursuit of sagacity requires considerable discipline of intellect and the activities of inquiry and attention; and the desires of the would-be sage must tolerate that kind of life. But sages may not have the will to do what they know they ought to or to desire what they know is worthy, beyond those things directly connected with attaining enlightenment.

Saintliness is a different matter. Whereas soldiers may force themselves to do something they do not like, saints do not come to like something without having the will to try it. An impulse of the heart which is rightly aimed but not sufficiently strong so as to organize the person's activity into full-blown public pursuit of its object is deficient as a desire. Jonathan Edwards called these feeble inclinations "mere wouldings." A properly developed desire *includes* the discipline of organizing activity in its pursuit. Will is included in well-developed desire; but desire of an object is not necessary for the organized will to pursue it. Likewise with respect to understanding, a properly developed desire aims at its right object. Genuinely to desire something is to understand it as the fulfillment of the desire's strivings. Perfected eros (in the Platonic sense) cannot have an end unworthy of being desired. Understanding is included in well-developed desire; but desire of an object is not necessary for the understanding that it ought to be desired. Sometimes the description of "saint" is given to people with ineffective and misguided but "sincerely" meant good wishes. This is a mistake; a saint is someone with heroic *accomplishments*, and the accomplishment of the heart's perfection requires both discipline and understanding.

As a philosophical prologue to the discussion of saintliness, it is necessary to say more about the nature of desires. Plato observed in the *Symposium* that eros is the mediating link between actual fact and ideals, between the process of becoming and the state of ideal being whose patterns guide process. Persons are not fixed facts but *movements* of facts. More specifically: persons are movements from one arrangement of facts to another. The limits of rearrangement are set by the nature of the earlier set of facts; they can be rearranged in only a limited number of diverse ways. But which way is taken in the movement is decided within the movement's process itself.

For personal action the process of selection is in part intentional. After whatever conscious or unconscious deliberation goes on, the rearrangement aimed at is intended, and the intention directs the process of reorganization. But the object intended is not ordinarily chosen simply because it is a possible rearrangement. Rather, it is viewed as better than the others, as more attractive, because it seems to have something the alternatives lack: its peculiar value. Desire is therefore a three-termed relation: the actual facts needing rearrangement in process, the pattern of rearrangement aimed at, and the value believed to be embodied in the goal, making the goal ideal. The value itself can be called an ideal, but only insofar as it can be imagined as having the shape of some rearrangement of affairs which would embody it.

In one sense people *are* their desires. That is, they are not their past states alone, nor merely the changing from the past to the new state, but rather the changing guided by the selection of their goals for their attractiveness. Of course, there are many desires in people's lives, coordinated by encompassing integrating desires; will and reason are aspects of the integration and selection of desires. This concept of desire is a basic philosophic notion. The past states of people are themselves the outcomes of processes directed by previous feelings for their attractiveness. And each component of the past states is the result of such a process.

This conception of desire differs from the drive model and from the instinct model. The drive model, as used by Freud, for instance, hypothesizes that there is a reservoir of energy under pressure to be let out. The energy seeks an outlet of expression. In his developmental theory Freud suggested that children channel their libidinal drives first to oral feelings, then to anal, and finally to genital sexuality. Sexual orgasm itself is the prime analogate in Freud's conception of the release of the pressure of energy: there is a build-up of tension to the point of climactically overflowing the dam, and then a feeling of greatly relaxed pressure. The aim of sexual pressure, on the drive model, is its extinction. The Platonic conception of eros as defended here can also take sex as the paradigm, but not the orgasm in isolation. The Platonic conception is that desire is drawn on by attractiveness in front, as it were, not pushed by a drive from behind. Being in love is the paradigm desire because it continually increases tension, bringing more and more elements of the people's experience into the relationship. Sexual acts are expressions of the communication of this intensity, and the sense of momentary exhaustion is just a part of the rhythm of life, not the goal of intercourse.

The instinct model, on the other hand, hypothesizes that people are pre-programed to desire certain things. They desire things, not because of the apparent attractiveness of those things, but because they are programed to see those things as attractive. The instinct theory is plausible for those who believe that no real values exist and that value-oriented behavior must come from creatures' projecting values onto things. But it is a ridiculous claim upon credibility to believe that every value felt in experience is a projected fiction. Furthermore, the instinct theory does not explain much. The instinctive reach for something is only a phenomenon to be understood, not an explanation for the existence of instinctive behavior.

On the theory that desires arise in response to a presented attractive object, it is necessary to say that desires are learned. The conscious desires of adults can be self-taught. That is, by reflecting on past experience, and imaginatively conceiving of new possibilities, people can think up new things to desire. By use of mental creativity they can construct new patterns which would integrate elements in life otherwise incompatible, and these can be desired and pursued as the conjoint fulfillment and mutual enhancement of the prior elements. But most desires are filled with unconscious elements, and these must be learned in dependence on the environment. Fetuses find the womb a source of many pleasurable sensations, and are born with desires for warmth and cuddling. As children grow, their experience is enriched with many patterns which organize and focus their lives, giving definiteness to their satisfactions (and avoidances). They learn the desirability of food, communication, and speech, or variety in visual and auditory stimuli, and so forth. The older they get the more they are able to suggest to themselves things to pursue in order to incorporate more attractions into life. They must be seduced into radically new desires, however. Seduction is the chief curriculum by which society civilizes its young to want the things truly worth having.

The instinct hypothesis correctly notes that basic instincts are common to all members of the species, and the desire theory must account for this. In the first place, the early experience of all people is common. We all start off in wombs, and therefore the early forms of desired pleasurable sensation are learned by common experience. Most infants are given nourishment by sucking through the mouth. (With the anticipated invention of artificial wombs perhaps there will be critical experiments testing whether desire for human contact is learned; maybe test tube babies will prefer warm baths to warm bodies! But then the artificial wombs may have to simulate the real ones so closely that a difference in sensation might not be discernible.) In the second place, individuals in a species have pretty much the same genetic makeup, and that genetic character plays a very significant role among the resources to be integrated in early fetal and infantile experience. After children are grown, their previous experience provides important elements to be integrated in desires, particularly the elements of which they are conscious. But for babies, desires must pull their bodies together, and baby bodies are very similar. Instinctive behavior is to be accounted for, on the desire theory, as a learned desire functioning to integrate mainly physiological processes in an environment similar to that shared by other young members of the species.

Because the physiological makeup of infants changes quickly according to genetic plan, there are some desires which must be learned within a definite short time if they are to be learned at all. Afterward there simply are not the physiological resources to be integrated in the desirable way. If a young cat is put in the dark and thus not allowed to discover the desirability of visual discrimination, after a certain point it can never learn to see when brought into the light. This is not important if the desires are not necessary for environmental adaptation or for the development of higher desires; but they often are.

Hardly any desire is important only for itself. Beyond very basic physical desires most desires themselves are integrated ways of combining other desires; without the integrating desire the separate ones could not be made compatible. On the other side, most desires are components of higher desires: they provide elements of the pattern out of which the higher desires are made. Also some of them provide the energy, each in the pursuit of its lower goal, for the pursuit of the higher.

Consider, for instance, mature sexual love between two people. Imagine the multifarious desires which must be learned for this love to be the real thing! Suppose, for instance, that Freud's theory of the oral, anal, and genital stages of infantile sexuality is mainly true, and that a particular person had a frustrated oral stage, say, with the result that he or she finds little pleasure as an adult in oral stimulation. That person may then profess pleasure in kissing, but the pleasure would not be genuinely felt; it would not be a feeling but a mere sentiment, a made-up feeling. Think how much more than erogenous stimulation is involved in mature sexual love! The lovers should have learned to desire the smells and the sights of bodies. They should take pleasure in the communication of intimacies involved in lovemaking, in playing with the boundaries of privacy. And for the love to be mature they should delight in the appreciation of all the things each brings to love—ambitions and frustrations, knowledge and skills, senses of self and desires for a life of love. Anyone who fails to feel these things and countless more, even if one can fake them, cannot be a mature lover. Fortunately the attempt at love is itself seductive enough to send many people back to fill in their missed feelings!

To grow into a mature human being is to develop a highly complex set of desires, interrelated in ways as multifarious as the circuitry of the brain and responsive to more nuances of the physical and social environment than could be named. Conscious reason is relevant only to the patterns of the highest and most sophisticated desires. Even will is limited in its potential affections. We must count on our bodies and societies to structure our desires from the roots to nearly the ends of the branches. (Given the mistakes of reason and perversities of will, the blind seduction of bios and polis is probably a blessed safeguard.)

It is hard enough to become an ordinary human being, functioning with a modicum of happiness in society and passing on to others the sense of worth necessary for life. To become a *good* citizen, a *Mensch*, is even more difficult, and mysterious as well. To become a saint is a miracle.

PERFECTION OF DESIRES

There is no lack of good advice about the basic things one ought to want. Of course, fitting those desirable ends into one's life may be a matter of some subtlety; casuistical deliberation is a difficult though necessary matter. But the main problem comes after one knows what one ought to want yet before one wants it enough. *Actions* can be made to conform to the dictates of reason by the vigorous exercise of will. But can one will oneself to *feel* what one ought?

To say that people are responsible for their feelings as well as for their actions is to suppose that they can have some control over feelings. By "feeling" here is meant the sensations of desires, the responses which one makes to things within and without oneself considered in light of their affective tone; one's "feelings about . . ." are how one values the thing immediately in one's own experience; these feelings stand in contrast to intellectual conclusions one might have reached out of the context of direct response about how the thing ought to be valued.

Consistent with the theory of desires described above, a feeling is, first of all, a direct response to the object, a grasp of the object itself or of some aspect of it. The feeling is formed in part by the object, and to say that one is responsible for *this* part is to deny the possibility of objective perceptive feelings. Some philosophers have gone so far as to take basic feelings to be certain and indubitable starting points for knowledge; if one has a toothache one feels the pain no matter how one wants to respond or what one does about it.

Still, two senses must be distinguished in which a thing can be felt to have value. It can be felt for itself, with its own affective tone. This is so even when the very perceiver is part of the subject matter felt. "My tooth really hurts!" "This party is depressing." "That sunset is sublime." "The price of freedom is constant struggle, but it's worth it!" On the other hand, the thing can be felt for how important perceivers will allow it to be within their own experience, how it contributes to the power or limitations of their own integrity and satisfaction. "My toothache blocks everything else from my mind." "This depressing party won't get me down." "The sunset restores my faith that peace overcomes tragedy." "The price of freedom is more than I am willing to pay now."

The first sense of feeling, that of discerning the object's own value or affective tone, is beyond the control of perceivers. But the second sense of feeling, wherein the object is given a value for one's own experience, is a function of the integration of that feeling with others, and integration *is* a matter of control! The will of saintly people is developed to bring control to their very feelings and desires. A desire can be conceived to be a feeling about some possibility whose subjective role within the person's experience is to organize that experience in pursuit of the possibility.

Of course, control over feelings and desires may never be complete. But through the many techniques of self-knowledge discussed before, from psychoanalysis to yoga, the character of many of those desires can be brought to consciousness. And by the exercise of disciplined will some can be developed and reinforced while others are set aside. The problem of taking responsibility for one's desires cannot be reduced, however, to manipulating already given psychic components. Desires are positive things, neither neutral nor automatically present. They must be given in experience, and that positive occurrence is dependent upon two factors: first, upon actually having the personal components which could be organized into the desire; and, second, upon meeting up with the ideal—either in imagination or in fact—which could be the organizing goal. Even if one's actual desires were understood, and understood in connection with what they ought rather to be, and if one's will were strong enough to inhibit and reinforce them, one still could not construct a desire which has not been given in experience. *The main problem in perfecting desires is missing or incomplete experience, not a surfeit of bad desires.*

One's emotional life ordinarily is a tangle of knots. Perhaps many of one's crucial early experiences, from which one would learn essential desires, were missing or frustrated or perverted in some way. By and large in early youth one is not responsible for the tangles in one's experience. One is not responsible for missing love which was never offered. And one is not responsible for the positive things in one's experience which prevented one from experiencing what one should have, the conflicts and contradictions of family life which make it seem miraculous that any of us survives! As one grows older, of course, one may choose one's own corruption, affirming desires for which one clearly has better alternatives; by adulthood one is responsible for reinforcing one's early character if there are any alternatives open.

Reason does indeed provide alternatives. As one can understand that one's tangles do consist in missing or distorted eros, so one can find ways to untangle one's emotions. One can find someone who will give one the infantile love one missed, a psychoanalyst, perhaps, engaging in transference; or simply a friend who is able to relate to one as an infant as well as an adult. One can seek out a community which will enable one to purify one's sense of dependence and independence, reforming one's growth within a family. One is lucky if one's society acknowledges these common needs and supplies remedies. But even if it does not, they can be sought out in unlikely places. Surely it is the responsibility of us all to understand our immaturity of desires and undertake the development necessary to come to maturity. And just as surely it is the responsibility of each of us to nurture our fellows.

The notion of responsibility for one's basic desires, for one's heart, is very important, and is perhaps a departure from common thinking about responsibility. A drunken man cannot control his driving and is therefore not as such responsible for the automobile accident which he causes. A woman who smokes is not responsible for dying of lung cancer. But the drunk is responsible for being drunk in the first place, and on that account can be held responsible for his driving. As the evidence for smoking as a cause of cancer becomes clearer, society is coming to believe that the smoker, who can control and therefore be responsible for her smoking, is likewise culpable for getting cancer in the first place. Both the drinker and the smoker *can* be held responsible for particular acts which they cannot control in the particular situation because the reason they lack control, i.e., drinking and smoking, is something which they can control. The control of desires is even more basic than this!

Suppose the drunk says he cannot control his drinking because he is an alcoholic, and the smoker her smoking because she is addicted to nicotine. But alcoholics can kick the habit with AA, and smokers with will power, if physiological dependence is the only problem. Usually it is not. Suppose the drunk is an alcoholic because he is profoundly depressed, and suppose the smoker is a reformed nailbiter who had an unsatisfactory oral development. Suppose both the depression and the infantile frustration were caused by others. The drunk and the smoker are not responsible for making themselves what they are. But they are responsible for remaining that way. At least they have the responsibility to attempt the cures—anti-depressive drugs and psychotherapy, abundant kissing, etc.—because they can control the means of cure.

But is this not arrogant nonsense, illustrating the absurdity of asserting responsibility for basic desires? A genuinely depressed drunk may not want to be cured! Even if his relatives haul him off to the clinic and he is forcibly "cured," the possibility of control and therefore the responsibility did not rest with him. Similarly, if the smoker could trust others to give her oral pleasure, she would not have the trouble in the first place.

Here we come to a crucial juncture regarding will. Tangled people choose to remain tangled. Given the past construction of their desires, they desire no other than what they have chosen, even when they understand intellectually what the alternatives are. They have no real alternative for choice. But paradoxically they would have an alternative if they chose it! At no point is it impossible to choose to be free.

But wait. The intellectually constructed alternative is not a genuine feeling, derived from direct experience, but a mere imagined sentiment. How can it be a *real* alternative?

The alternative is not the alternate desire but the reconstruction of experience which would give flesh to that desire and untangle the knots. That is, the people must choose the cure. They must choose to search for the healing person and nurturing community. Not to choose this is to affirm that there is no hope.

Of course, for many deficiencies of experience there is no hope indeed! Reconstructive techniques such as psychoanalysis and yoga are primitive. Some individuals may search for psychic healing all their lives and simply never find the right people. The question of hope is in some measure an empirical one. But at its most profound it is not an empirical question for the people who need hope. For if they had the experience which would show that hope is justified—and that might be nothing more than a healing experience itself—then they indeed would not be hopeless. They would have chosen a path to recovery. An experience which justifies is one in which a person or technique for cure is not merely presented but presented in such a way that some degree of cure is accepted.

With the issue of hope we move from the ordinary vicissitudes of people seeking mature experience to the problems of spiritual liberation. Most people never reach a rock bottom, such as the profoundly depressed person does, in which there is no hope. Those who approach it may be jollied along by an analyst, friend, or preacher who evokes the strength to return from the path toward hopelessness. But for those who have reached rock bottom there is no strength left to be evoked by the blandishments of finite cheer and encouragement. The cosmos may indeed offer no hope, and even if it is offered, people at rock bottom cannot accept it.

This is the crisis of despair, and it should be attended to properly. One who feels absolutely hopeless should be aware of one's despair. If one has no hope and *complains* about it, then one is deceiving oneself in the belief that one has no hope. Genuine hopelessness is resignation. Most people who claim to be hopeless are really merely desirous of being helpless. That is, they want to be infants and to have someone else take their responsibility. Of course, if others do take that responsibility, perhaps the people will reform their early experience and take hope. But if this is possible, they were not without hope in the first place and were using the rhetoric of despair to gain sympathy and parental-like help.

Genuine despair is neutral resignation. The significance of this is that one is at the juncture at which one relinquishes the importance of all relations understood cosmologically and faces only the absolute existence of things. Things are not important for helping or hurting one, only for being what they are. The same is true of oneself. If one laments a blow to one's narcissism, then one still has hope, however ill-founded, in the benefits of one's egoism. If one is genuinely hopeless, nothing matters.

If despair reaches the point of pure indifference, what is one to do? The world is around one, with its absolute nature and its relative connections, partial and inadequate as they are. That world naturally presents itself to one. Not to see it requires the effort of blocking it out. But why should one block it out? If there is any *reason* to do so, then one's life has not reached hopelessness. Genuine despair would abandon rancor and rejection and allow the world to present itself. The issue then is, how does the world present itself?

When one is in despair, one sees the world as having absolutely no human interest. This is a true vision. The world, considered absolutely, has no human interest, in the sense that none of its connections is viewed as specially connected according to people's intentions. Considered cosmologically, this is an exaggeration; a table of food has the interest of being a meal, and in despair one might not deny this even though one would deny that it has any ultimate significance. When one's friends show one all the little connections and benefits which grace one's life with their partial meanings, without hope one might say, "but there is nothing of ultimate interest, no ultimate meaning, no ultimate hope in perfection, and without ultimate interests, the partial interests are as good as nothing!" One would be right; the cosmological connections of the world have no ultimate human interest, only relative interests.

But when in despair, let one consider something absolutely; anything will do—one's room, one's fantasies, the river running past one's city. Whatever object one considers has a complex structure defining it. It has components unique to itself, and components by virtue of which it differs from things other than itself. Its own structure is the way in which those components are harmonized. Perhaps those components could be harmonized in a better way than the one which actually appears, perhaps in worse ways. But at any rate any structure has some value embodied in the way in which it harmonizes its components. To be a structure is to have some value, even if a low degree, even if such a low degree that in its cosmological context it is a deficit, an evil. If in despair one looks indifferently on one's world, one must appreciate it as good absolutely. (From the relative standpoint, the world's values may add up to nothing, vanity. Or they may be positively wicked relative to human interests, although this is too much "meaning" for one in real despair to admit.)

The position claimed here—that everything in the world, absolutely considered, is good in some degree—is ancient but by no means universal. It received clearest expressions in Western creationist philosophies in which there is a motive to say that everything which God creates is good. It received widest apparent denial in Buddhism, the main drift of which is to say that dharmas are value-neutral in every respect, absolute as well as relative. It is necessary to say more in defense of the position.

Consider the following analogy. In a temporal activity one employs means to achieve a certain goal. The goal is a valuable state of affairs (or is believed to be) and the means employed are the ways of actualizing the value. We have sometimes been inclined to think that the goal is external to the means, for instance, later. But, as John Dewey pointed out, the actual value achieved is the sum total of the values involved, positively and negatively, in the entire process. The value gain or loss in a human activity is not the end state considered apart from any means which might have achieved it, nor even the end state considered as the summation of the means. It is the sum of the values in the whole process, including the values of immediate experience felt along the way, values which dwell only in a finite time and which cannot be summed up in a later time—for instance, the values of suffering and the joy of working. The structure of a human activity is such that a human interest is served by the end of the activity as arranged by the earlier stages. Yet the value of the activity is not just the human interest achieved at the end but the values ingredient in the process read discursively from beginning to end; a properly self-conscious human interest would include an approval of the value of the whole as well as that of the end sought (although few interests are *that* reflective of their costs).

Now suppose—and here is the analogy—that a creator were acting in a non-temporal way so as to cause his or her end immediately. (Think of the old-fashioned image of God creating the world.) This immediate causation has no early stages which give direction and meaning to the end by which it would be possible to read the maker's intentions from the direction of the process. There would only be the end made. The immediacy of this kind of causation is such that there are no components *before* the causal activity which are recombined to produce the end. Like the ordinary human activity, however, there is a value in the end. In fact, the structure of the end is the means whereby the value is embodied or achieved. Just as the ordinary activity arranges a structure so that the value intended will be embodied, the immediate activity makes structure as the embodiment of a certain value. The difference is that with the ordinary activity it is possible to read out from the early stages the end at which the activity is aimed, a possibility lacking in a non-temporal activity. The likeness in the analogy is that in both cases structure is appreciated as the means of embodying value. Or perhaps, to remove the temporal connotations of means–ends language, the structure is the vehicle in which value is actual.

The absolute existence of the world as structured is valuable. Any of its parts has some value carried by its structure. The real value of an ordinary human activity is the sum of all the values in the process of its unfolding, including but not limited to the summation value of the end achieved; that is, the real value of the activity is its absolute value. To say, as we did, that a properly self-conscious human interest ought to include an interest in the values involved in the means of attaining an end is only to say that such a proper interest ought to include the absolute as well as the relative appreciation of things. Put more accurately: the relative values in human affairs are included in the absolute values when the entire context and process comprise the structure regarded absolutely.

The person in despair must interject at this point. The very reason for despair is that "ordinary human activity" is a myth, at least in important cases. People seriously misjudge the values of the ends which they intend; their interests are not what they think. Their activities employ the wrong means; they fail to accomplish their goals and they usually accomplish all sorts of unlooked-for ends (mainly those whose values are quite contrary to human interests). And when it comes to the genuinely important kinds of activity—those of building character, of perfecting the desires, for instance—the activities simply disintegrate and fall apart. It is vain to think that people can get themselves together to accomplish anything significant.

Things are probably not as bad as despair often leads one to think. But even if they were, the point still holds: the things in the world, whether or not they add up so as to accomplish particular human interests, still have value absolutely in themselves. If, in despair, one were to abandon all human interest and to adopt as one's own the divine interest—that is, the appreciation of the values of things absolutely—one's world would still be filled with value.

But wait. The argument so far that structures are ipso facto valuable has been very metaphysical, even analogical. A person without hope cares nothing for this. The value must be *palpable* even to those who have no interest in finding value.

The answer to this, of course, must be experiential. Putting aside all special interests, one must open one's eyes and see! But this is no argument.

An argument can be given, however, as to why this kind of experience might be expected. Considered from the aesthetic standpoint of sheer appreciation, why is a structure valuable? It is valuable because it combines diversity with unity. In diversity it is able to include the values of many things; in unity it is able to include them together. Its variety gives it complexity; its unity gives it simplicity. There are degrees of value, of course. A thing is more valuable when, without sacrificing simplicity, it increases in complexity, combining a greater variety of diverse things. It is also more valuable when, without sacrificing complexity, it increases simplicity, basing its integration on purer and simpler principles which are more fruitful for combining and recombining the variety of components. The greater the harmony, the more complexity and simplicity are maximized together. But there can be no formula for such a mixture. Rather, there is an aesthetic "elegance" to structures, the grasp of which is the appreciation of its value. Elegance, in the sense in which I mean it here, is the way by which simplicity and complexity are combined to intensify the integration of various components. The more elegant the structure, the more each component is enhanced just by being in the structure.

Elegance is what a mathematician looks to in choosing the better of two valid proofs. The nature and degree of simplicity and complexity are what a connoisseur looks to in assessing a work of art. The moralist looks for the simplest way of working out a conflict in values so that all parties lose least and gain as much as possible. Is not evaluation in all areas of experience a matter of illuminating the complexities and possibilities for simple integration in the harmonies perceived or imagined? What this suggests is that the appreciation of any structure involves the grasp of its harmony as having a value. Simply to perceive a structured thing, prescinding from the disappointments or personal satisfactions which might attend an antecedent special interest, is to grasp it as valuable in *its* way.

If one's despair is pure and not alloyed with unabandoned hopes, one perceives any part of the world coming to one's attention in its absolute value.

What has been traced here is the attainment of the absolute standpoint with respect to values. Quite apart from any spiritual ambition regarding the perfection of one's desires, even with a plainly secular life, one might be driven to despair. But if so, and if one goes all the way, one perceives the world's absolute value as it comes before one. This is to say, apart from any spiritual ambition, in despair one finds oneself in a spiritual dimension of life. One's experience becomes significant not in its cosmological relations—in despair that dimension is meaningless—but in its character as absolute.

This is also the beginning for spiritual seekers, ambitious to perfect their desires. Of course, would-be saints need not abandon appreciation of various relative human interests; they need not have despair which leads to renunciation of interested activity. But they must come to appreciate the values of things in their absolute characters. They must attain to the indifference of despair, and actual despair has been an effective vehicle for this. Having attained indifference, they must renounce the *need* for any guarantee of viable human interests. If experience shows that they are possible and worthy—contrary to the view of the person in despair—so much the better; but if not, the absolute values are still to be appreciated in themselves.

To perfect their desires, saints must not only appreciate the objects of their desires in their absolute values, but also must see their very desiring in its absolute value. In doing this they abandon any attachment to their values as the interests of their ego, and merely observe that they are the interests of their own intentions. Those interests, such as they are, have an absolute value which may be appreciated. Without abandoning special interest in the objects of their own desires, would-be saints are not free to perfect them.

The next step, of course, is to ask whether the particular desires are the best possible. This takes the form of asking whether the large-scale integrating desires are as they should be. The difference between would-be saints asking this question and ordinary people limited to relative viewpoints, is that the former have as their ultimate criterion the enhancement of the values of things absolutely considered. In Jonathan Edward's phrase, they have "benevolence to being in general." Now, among the things most directly in their attention is their own characters, including their desires. But what measures the perfection of these desires is not their personal interests in perfecting them but the general enhancement of values absolutely.

Saints may well have to abandon any particular image of a "perfect desire," because perfection in this context means desiring the perfection of the world. Except for fairly general traits such as benevolence, saints' desires may be not much different in appearance from those of others; they are just the right ones in the right places. Of course, the way by which saints integrate their desires is distinctive; they come together with a particularly focused passion.

Discerning what harmonies are properly to be desired is a task of reason. A healthy eros is one aiming at its relative end within the context of things considered absolutely, and this is most difficult to discern. Although the grasp of the absolute values of things may be intuitive, discernment of how to enhance them is surely not.

After initial attainment of the indifference from which values can be seen absolutely, the will must go on to shape the selective reinforcement and elimination of desires in accord with what would perfect them. This too is a step-by-step process in which backsliding is doubtless the rule.

As remarked before, the possibility of having improved desires depends on having the experiences which allow them to be felt genuinely. Ways must be found to fill in the experiences which untangle the knots inhibiting genuine desires. But perhaps there are no ways. Suppose there is no cure. Then the saints must come to terms with limiting the perfection of their desires to what is possible within the relativities of their world. Perhaps one is incapable of mature sexual love, and there is no remedy for this. One must still come to desire those things which are possible which best enhance the values of the world absolutely. One's personal experience will seem frustrated. But then one has already abandoned one's ego in despair and appreciates one's limited experience for the small value it holds. Precisely because one has abandoned one's ego, however, in saintly commitment one is perhaps more open than others to attempt the experiences which may enrich one's capacity for desire.

The paradox in the perfection of desires is that such perfection entails the abandonment of the search for perfection in any egoist sense. Saints give up on perfecting many of their desires long before secular egoists realize that their strivings to become super people are vain. The perfection of desires begins with abandoning the special interest of having perfect desires. The saints' motive is not self-improvement but service to the desirability of the enhancement of things absolutely.

PERFECTION OF LOVE

The distinction between desire and love is not made with consistency in the ordinary ways we think. Most often love is thought to be an intense sort of desire, and sometimes we think to limit "love" to human objects (one who "loves" his automobile is thought to have a perverted kind of sexual love whose object ought to be human).

There is an important distinction to be singled out, however, and the words "desire" and "love" can mark the difference. Attraction to a valued object organizes activity for the goal of enjoying, achieving, maintaining, or enhancing the object. That organization may be pragmatically circumscribed; only those elements of one's existence which are relevant for pursuing the goal are involved in the organization, and the other elements, if affected at all, are only made compatible with the organization. These attractions may be called "desires," plain and simple. There are other attractions, however, in which the organization of oneself is a total mobilization; even those elements which are not relevant to the pursuit of the object are realigned because one transforms one's own whole identity into being a lover. This is love. Because desire is commonly taken to be the generic term, love can be called the special kind of love in which the image of the whole self is as much to be acted upon as the image of the desired object.

An object of love is prized for itself. An object of desire is prized because it harmonizes or fulfills a plurality of things which the desirers antecedently prize, often mainly elements of their own lives and situations. Lovers, however, are themselves fulfilled in the prized service of their beloved, even at the risk of sacrifice of the things usually thought to be parts of their identity and world. The transition from desire to love is crucial for would-be saints.

Consider sexual desire. People are constituted with tensions which come together in satisfaction only with sexual activity. Sexual object choice is learned through a vastly complex process of discovering desires which intensify rather than repel and dissociate experience. Some choose themselves; some choose others of the same sex; some choose those of the opposite sex. At its crudest level, as manifested in locker-room talk, for instance, these choices are aimed at classes of objects, not particular people. That is, any woman, any man will do. (An exception to this might be the autoerotic person whose character is extraordinarily narcissistic; but most exclusive autoeroticism results from a fear of engaging other people, and so sex with oneself is really sex with the class of non-others!) The classes may be more narrowly qualified: blond women, he-men, etc.

But real sexual activity is always with individuals. Consider heterosexual lovemaking. Even extraordinarily promiscuous people have difficulty bearing in mind that their partner is only a "body of the right class." It is conceivable that some people are able so to fragment themselves as to have sexual relations indifferently with people in their preferred class without emotional attachments or any reference to individual characters. But most folk include within the makeup of their sexual desires a need to have their own sexual status—their attractiveness or prowess—acknowledged and appreciated. In our culture there are learned stereotypes of how to feed one's partner's sexual ego. Women learn to complement brute sexual strength by playing dumb and offering no competition in other areas of life. Men learn to turn women on with glances of calculated lewdness. But even with all the stereotypes which provide the exchanges of sexual affection necessary for copulation at its crudest, there would be an obvious enrichment if sexual appreciation also were sensitive to the individuality of the person one is with.

At a low level of attention to individuals, sexual desire may still be selfish. One may be attracted to another person over and beyond physical appreciation because the other satisfies (or contradicts) one's individual needs for specific things. One's economic situation may profit from a partner of a certain class; parents and friends have particular expectations; one may have idiosyncratic interests of one's own for which a particular person is singularly appropriate. But at this level the person whose individuality is recognized is the would-be lover, not the would-be beloved. The beloved is appreciated because he or she belongs to a very narrow class of individuals fulfilling one's unique individual needs for a human partner, sexual and otherwise.

On a higher level is the recognition of the other as an individual. This sometimes comes as a shock, and is not always followed by love of what is recognized. In the early stage of acquaintance in the case of those who desire sexual partners, each may come to recognize the individual traits of the other, approving some and being reconciled to others. Each may view the other as a unique person, not exchangeable with any other, who after a while may become historically defined in terms of the mutual relationship. This may include various forms of projecting oneself into how the other thinks and feels. But there may come a time when the other is recognized not primarily as an individual who is desired for the sum of his or her traits but primarily as an individual as such, with a subjectivity of his or her own and before whom one appears as a potential individual. At this point one faces two potential centers for one's own experience: one's own and the other's. One views the other individual as a potential center for organizing the world, including oneself. The other's desires are placed in competition with one's own.

This is a crucial decision point. Either the subjective individuality of the other must be suppressed, and the relationship fixed merely at a high level of desire, or the satisfaction of the other must be willed as one had previously willed one's own. If the latter decision is made, one has become a lover. The desire for the other has been transformed into a desire to remake oneself for the other's satisfaction. One abandons giving priority to one's own interests and transforms them into what is hoped will serve the beloved's interests.

But why would one do this? The selfish desire to make oneself a lover, because lovers are better than others? This would require using the other as a tool, and could only be a fake love. There could be no open entry into the interests of the other person. What is the motive for real love?

At this point of displacement into another's subjectivity, one perceives, however vaguely or mistakenly, the other's subjective feeling for an ideal. Each person's subjective life is a matter of pursuing ideals, or concrete goals embodying ideals, in relation to actual facts and accomplishments. Love begins when one feels the other's subjective feeling for ideals. This is beyond feeling what the other's ideals are and knowing how the other pursues them, both of which are objective facts and can be appreciated on the level of desire alone.

Included among one's ideals is, or ought to be, a composite ideal for oneself; this is an ideal self-image. Plato, in the *Phaedrus*, put the point in terms of divine character. There are many different types of people, he said, and for each type there is a god perfecting the type. One of the tasks of life is to discern who one's god is and to follow it. In loving, one sees one's beloved in the subjective pursuit of the god. The attractiveness of the god is the super motivation which moves one from desire to love, on Plato's account. From pursuing the beloved for his own attractiveness, the root of which is sex, one moves to pursuing the beloved's god.

Plato's conclusion from this was that one tries first to be like the beloved, and then like the beloved's god. Although this perhaps is true in lovers who are rather alike to begin with, something else takes place too (or instead). In willing the other's satisfaction, one wills that the other become perfected in the image of his or her god. That is, one as lover wills the perfection of the other. Then as to oneself, one wills that one may serve the beloved's perfection.

What does this mean in less ideal terms? Most people have not found their muse to begin with. They do not have a consistent ideal image for themselves, and may be in the process either of working this out or of running from it. Therefore, in willing the perfection of the other, one needs first to help the beloved find himself or herself. The guiding ideals for personal idiosyncratic development may not easily be symbolized in a divine type (at least not by us who are so ill-adept at polytheism). The ideals of a soldier, sage, and saint are far too general to give individual identity to a person's strivings. But people who know themselves and have found their ideals, even changing them through stages of maturity, can project a sense of identity consisting in a mixture of the ideals. They have a sense of development and of what this might mean in concrete life in terms of sacrifices and contributions; in short, their lives are drawn by lineaments of an ideal career, however much the ideal changes with new experience. In loving, one helps one's beloved find and be guided by such a sense of identity.

But what does this mean for one as lover? Of course, even at the first rush of feeling one imagines oneself helping concretely. One's fantasies abound, in which one rescues or spectacularly supports the beloved in something relevant to the beloved's ideal pursuits. But a special problem inevitably arises. Even as lover one is a person, and cannot forever exhaust one's identity in roles of service to the beloved. In fact, since any genuine ideal of perfection requires that one become a lover, in loving, one wills the beloved to become a lover too (one might hope to be included among the beloved objects). So one must transform oneself from a lover in fact to a lover in ideal for the beloved. As a lover in fact, one is determined by one's will of the perfection of the other, and one determines oneself to will this, instead of one's own interest, with all one's heart. As a lover in ideal, one's identity is that of pursuing the ideal of being a lover, of the beloved in particular. As lover in fact, one is determined by the beloved. As lover in ideal, one is determined by one's own ideal, which is partly relevant to the beloved; being a lover in ideal includes and transcends being a lover in fact.

One of love's greatest paradoxes appears here. In order to give full love to a beloved, one must be sufficiently self-possessed and determined in one's intrinsic character as a lover so as not to need to give love to the beloved. At this point, love becomes a gift to the beloved, not the expression of a need. Desire is transformed into grace.

Until one is free from the need to love, loving is always using the other person for the satisfaction of one's higher desires. This is true even in that subtle sense in which one has transformed one's own desires into the desires of the other for the other's ideal. A more complete love is given when it does not have to be given. Such freedom requires a saintly perfection of one's own character as a lover.

As a lover one is able to will the perfection of the beloved without having to be involved in this process in order to be satisfied. As lover one must be secure in oneself so that one does not need to love in order to be satisfied. Then one can give one's love with no strings attached. Like the beloved, one must discover and follow one's own god; one must be secure and independent in one's own self. Contrary to Plato's suggestion, lover and beloved need not follow the same god; in fact, that should be a matter of indifference except in matters of household convenience.

In concrete life one learns to be a lover in segmented lessons. The strings of attachment are untied one at a time as the tiers of a secure character are built. Being loved by someone else is for most of those strings a condition for their detachment. One needs to love another in a certain respect until the other loves the root of that need, at which point one becomes free there. Philosophical conceptions simply cannot describe the intricacy of the ways by which two people lead each other to become greater lovers. There is always something unique in each relationship because of the historical contingencies under which people live. It seems clear, however, that many years are required in the process and much close living. The arguments that genuine love requires family life still have much weight.

Are saints merely advanced lovers? At least. But there is another dimension to saintly love. Secular lovers view both the beloved and themselves in terms of their cosmological relations, each defined in terms of his or her own world. Projection of their will into the center of the other, desiring the other's perfection from the standpoint of the other's subjectivity, is the closest they come within the cosmological perspective to appreciating something for its absolute self. At this point love borders on the divine perspective. But secular lovers need not take the next, the saintly, step of assuming the beloved's center of experience simply because the beloved exists. Saints love things for their absolute existence, not out of their own interest.

The chief mark of difference between enhanced secular love and saintly love is that the latter can love the unlovely. Ordinarily love begins with the beauty and attractiveness of the potential beloved, often in a sexual sense. Eros starts with the object's attractiveness. Although saints love in this way, and learn love this way, they finally become free to give love to those who are not attractive at all. At best, their absolute existence is cosmologically repulsive. Yet love means the same cosmologically or absolutely: it means the willing of the perfection of the other according to the other's relevant ideals. There is nothing in the world which is not a harmony of some sort; and there is nothing therefore for which there are not ideal modes of harmony, whether those are embodied or only imaginable. Saints can love every existent by willing its perfection. They love not only the lovely people but the unlovely, and not only people but everything within creation.

Mature love, secular or saintly, has an unexpected toughness. The first blush of love is a passion by which one's every aspect is overwhelmed by feelings about the beloved—the impulse of projection, the desire to please, the giddy joy of being transported beyond oneself. Mature love is settled enough to demand that the beloved discover and live up to his or her ideal. There is a terrible risk of offense here, since most of us would rather be fawned upon than chided to improve ourselves, and would for this reason refuse to requite such demanding love. As lovers we might very well refuse to be so demanding. But true love requires those demands. A lover makes those demands through seduction, of course, but sometimes seduction fails and one must simply stand firm. If one still *needs* to love at this point, one will be tempted to cave in if the beloved threatens rejection.

To be free from the need to love does not mean that the heartaches of love are any less. In fact, such freedom allows ever greater involvement, and one's emotions are in correspondingly greater jeopardy. Even if one does not love out of need, being rejected causes pain and anguish beyond measure. But as a free lover one can bear that pain and anguish, and in fact will choose it where it means the integrity of one's love, but the person who loves out of need will flee as long as possible anything which would cause the pain.

Christian sacrificial love and the bodhisattva's postponement of Nirvāṇa indicate saintly transformation of oneself into a lover. As saint one acts not to satisfy desires which may characterize one or one's personally defined world, but to perfect all the beings whom one loves in the pursuit of their own ideals. One may think of oneself in this regard; but love of oneself would be willing one's perfection as a lover, since this is one's ideal. And so as saint one is turned out to the world again. If loving demands the neglect or sacrifice of one's personal fortunes, so be it. If loving demands the sacrifice of one's own life, one would be wary indeed of the argument which suggests loving less fully now so as to be around to love better later.

With regard to love, saintly reason has a special problem. Assuming that sagacity tells one what to love and what one's love should will (that is, how one's beloved should pursue the relevant ideals) as saint one must still evoke that pursuit. The greatest danger of saintliness is authoritarianism. Should one force the beloved to improve? Since freedom is at the base of most human ideals, as saint one must lead the beloved to choose well. Seduction is a process which divides responsibility for change. The seducer blocks the beloved's usual defenses and intensifies the attractiveness of what he or she wants the beloved to choose. But because the beloved's character as a voluntary agent is respected and encouraged by the seducer, the beloved is still responsible for choosing. The greatest prudence is required to do this. As saint one errs either by thinking the decision is one's own in the first place or by overloading the demands on the beloved's freedom. Living with a saint is perhaps more grueling than being one!

The powers of saintliness are greatly to be feared. More than other people saints are able to will with undistractible consistency, to understand how to do what they want, and to conform their desires so exactly to the direction of their will that the tendency of their passion is overwhelmingly reinforced and not conflicted. A small mistake of saintly reasoning can unleash a mighty power for harm. If a misdirected soldier is dangerous, a mistaken saint is close to Satan!

Saintly power is dangerous beyond the misdeeds of the saint. The response which one evokes in others is quite literally beyond one's will. Of course, as a *sage* saint one will understand how others are likely to respond to displays of one's virtues and power, and can guard against the likelihood of envy and wicked rejection. But likelihood does not cover all the relevant bases. Individuals respond in definite existential judgments, not without the influence of environmental pressures but sometimes in opposition. As a saint one cannot take responsibility for the person whose will is turned wicked by the confrontation with one's love. As John Milton laid bare in *Paradise Lost*, there are some, whose powers and virtues are indeed great, who choose to turn to evil in the face of even greater power and goodness. To understand the tragedy of this, not on the plains of heaven but in our own lives, it is necessary to call to attention the powers attendant on the accomplished saint.

The desires of most of us are compatible but not coordinated. They fit together more or less in the same life. But the price of that fit is segmentation of life. Furthermore, most of us cannot pour all our energies into the pursuit of any one desire because there are others deflecting the energy. We are not able to feel our love for family, for instance, with the same passion with which we pursue the values of career, and therefore divide our passions between them with only partial reinforcement. Saints' desires are coordinated, however, so that the pursuit of any one is at the same time the pursuit of all the others. The energy in one serves all, and the energy of all can be turned to any one. Of course, in finite people no matter how saintly, this is always a matter of degree, but saints have this accomplished to a high degree. Not only can they "will one thing," in Kierkegaard's phrase, but they know and want one thing.

Spiritual literature of all traditions is filled with stories of the special powers saints have transcending ordinary natural ones. These are the *siddhis*, the special accomplishments which are not so much contraventions of nature as enhancements of nature to contravene ordinary outcomes. We need not believe the more extravagant claims to understand how it might be possible to draw upon the fundamental powers of the universe, setting them free from their usual channels. The human sphere, properly pursued, transforms and intensifies the natural powers so as to increase the harmonies of nature rather than to limit them by human opposition.

True saints, sages, and soldiers coordinate their desires and love not for the sake of coordination but because of the attractiveness of a genuinely coordinating goal. Power is the result of the coordination, and the coordination is the result of loving the right things. Jonathan Edwards' definition of true virtue, in *The Nature of True Virtue*, marks out the saints' goals. "True virtue most essentially consists in *benevolence* to *being in general*. Or perhaps, to speak more accurately, it is that consent, propensity and union of heart to being in general, which is immediately exercised in a general good will."[1] As will be evident, this is the same as saying that the saints' overriding desire is a love of each existing thing as regards its absolute existence. Although Edwards' own theory of "being" involves more than has been argued here, the important part of his definition is the distinction between consent, propensity, and union of heart.

Consent, propensity, and union are all qualifications of heart, that is, of the inclinations or desires. Although "benevolence" literally means "good will," for Edwards it practically means "good heart." The very content of saintly life is to consent to, have a propensity for, and seek union with being in general.

The consent of the heart means that the desires are sensitive to, properly know, literally "feel with," the object of benevolence. There is also the connotation of agreement. "I see what you are, and say that's fine." The Lord consented to his creation when it was made, according to Genesis. This is to make the point already expressed above: in love or benevolence one sets aside one's personal desires and notes and desires the perfection of the beloved's nature.

The propensity of the heart distinguishes the cognitive side of desires from the inclining or moving. The energy in benevolence inclines toward being in general. In Edwards' scheme in one way, and in the position expressed above in another, the inclination toward the perfection of one being is not inconsistent with the inclination toward the perfection of all beings insofar as they potentially are in concord.

The union of heart is perhaps the most important qualification. This refers to the function of will in desiring. Union of heart to being in general means not only that one integrates one's own personal elements in the pursuit of the good of being, but also that one's personal elements themselves are integrated with the rest of being. Union of heart to being in general means that there is a union to all effort, not separate wills. Put another way: saints view their own efforts not as integral wholes within a system of other figures, but simply as integral parts of a larger universe of love. Union of heart to being in general means that there is but one agent ultimately, the totality of being.

Saints have their power by loving things in regard to their absolute existence: they love them as beings, in their ontological natures. Were they to love only cosmologically, even should they thoroughly love some other or even the whole world, freely and without the need to love, they would still have artificial limitations of the power of their love. For the things which are unlovely, and which in the cosmological view would be ignored, hated, or appreciated only in purely instrumental ways, would be lacunae in saintly benevolence. Saints love any being simply because it is.

From the standpoint of others, saints are dangerous because they have attained some accomplishment in what each of us feels would make us perfect. Love is the most intense of desires and the most powerful. As lover one holds within one's will all the powers available through nature at the time, and uses them to put one's own desires aside and to perfect the world for its own sake, insofar as it is available to one. In contrast to the non-lovers, saints have (ideally) perfect power over themselves. Saints may therefore be envied by the rest of us, not because of the purity and effects of their love, but because of their power, particularly over themselves. For we all know that we are our own worst enemies. Remember the rancor of the Romans and Jews toward Jesus, offended by the allegations of his perfection even if they were true. The offense of perfection provokes envy; with the knowledge that one cannot possess the power oneself, the envy turns to sadistic hate.

Yet for others saints are measuring rods. Of course, we are unsaintly and we envy the saints' virtuous powers. But in quiet moments the saintly image helps in judging what we are; without that judgment there can be no progress toward self-possession. Without saints around, however hopeless our own ambitions, a sense for our own ideals will always be vague.

From their own standpoint, the saints' danger is that they will forget the ontological foundations of the objects of their love. There is no contradiction between loving beautiful things for their beauty and loving them because they are. But one can forget to love the unlovely things for their existence, and they then will not be loved at all. The only love which resonates with the power of existence is the love of being in general. The saints' danger is not that they will be seduced from benevolence to being by the attractiveness of particular things, but that the habit of measuring things by their attractiveness will displace their love of being in general. The essence of saintliness is increasing faithfulness to being.

PERFECTION OF DIVINE COMMUNION

What is the relation between saints and God, or the absolute foundation of things? If we could apply a cosmological metaphor to God and call him a lover, or a loving creator, the relation would be that saints love what God loves, but only within the limits of their purview. They wish what God wishes within the limits of their sagacity. And they pursue God's ends, although with only those elements of natural power which can be focused at their finite times and places. But we cannot apply such metaphors to God precisely because they refer to definite created things and God is the creator of the whole, or the abyss whence arises the world as it is. Therefore the relation must be stated more abstractly.

Of that part of the world coming within their purview, saints delight in it the way God does, to the extent they grasp it. There are relative values in the world, some differing instrumentally and some intrinsically. But each thing, or any conceivable collection of things, is some finite achievement of value. God delights in the value of things simply as they exist, and, of course, the saints' love leads them to do the same.

To be sure, the metaphor here must be corrected because of the difference between human and divine delighting. People delight by mediating the delightful object into their own experience. God, not being a separate actuality with spatially and temporally distinct experience, has delight simply and only in the act of creating definite things. God's delight is in the delightfulness of his creating. Creating is delighting. An atheist expression of these things is to remark that the world, absolutely, is lovely: this is a remark about the world considered in its absolute character. Humans have something like this delight-in-creating as expressed in saying that a girl is her parents' "delight." This is different from saying that they reflect on the child and take delight in her. On the other hand, a child exists separately from her parents, and it is difficult for parents to sustain the delight-in-creation. The world does not exist separately from its creative ground, and hence God cannot exist subjectively over against it to delight in it privately; divine delight is not private.

As delight is the fulfillment of desire, accomplishment is the fulfillment of will, where "accomplishment" means the integration of elements so as to produce something. The existence of the world itself is the fulfillment of the will of God; since that will has no process within itself of earlier and later stages, the created product is the entire determinate character of the divine will, which produces its effect immediately.

There are two main senses in which human voluntary lives can be said to be aspects of God's will. First, any person's will, in fact any causal factor whatsoever, is a part of the way God accomplishes the creation. This is to be understood by recalling the distinction between ontological and cosmological causation. Anything which exists is caused to be itself by God; this is its ontological foundation. But *what* it is depends on its cosmological connections. For instance, rain is what it is because of a prior condensation of moisture in the atmosphere. God can only cause rain ontologically by also causing prior condensation ontologically; cosmologically, the condensation (and other factors) causes the rain. Or again, God can cause a mature free person to exist, but only by also causing the prior conditions of free choice to exist. Again, God can cause a victory for the forces of good against evil, but only by causing the development of power in the good forces. And the evil in their opponents. Now with reference to God's creation of the rain, the mature person, and the victory of goodness, the condensation, the prior choices establishing maturity, and the developed power of goodness are aspects of the divine creative will. If we could only be sure that God's world has a dramatic plan to it such that all leads to a specific end of the sort persons might be interested in, we could say that all existing causes are instruments of providence.

Second, a person's voluntary life might have an intention to love the world as such, as a special qualification over and above that in the previous paragraph. Saints have a conscious and affective sense of participating in the creation. Whereas cosmological causes contribute to the divine creation in their very causing, whether they know it or want to, saints add a dimension of *intending* the perfection of creation in their activity. They then may feel a special concord between their finite projects and the dynamic existence of the world. Of course, their activity is all cosmological, and they may in fact contribute no more than do the people oblivious to the ontological dimensions of things. But the quality of saintly experience is richer, and if they are at all sagacious they can act with greater resolution and selflessness than ordinary folk to prosper the creation.

Although the relation between God and the world is eternal and immediate, God being equally close to any being no matter what its place in the cosmological process, the relation between things in the world is temporal and mediated in countless ways. From one's standpoint within time, the knowledge that God is the immediate cause of some anticipated event does not lessen one's responsibility to act with respect to that event.

If saints approximate identity with God in the delight of their desires and the ontological intentions of their will, is there an identity in their knowledge? In one sense, of course, even the most accomplished of saints have finite knowledge, knowing only those things which come within their historical purview and with only such accuracy as can be mustered by people with their resources. In this they do not have perfect knowledge. So we may simply say that human knowledge is fallible even at its best.

In another sense, however, as a person, one has an experience of the world as a whole, not just those parts which one discriminates clearly or personally relates to. This experience may be mainly unconscious, and it surely is mediated by very general concepts. The sagacity of the saints gives a philosophical qualification to their experience of the world, not the philosophy of professional academics perhaps, but a wise grasp of the world as a whole. Saints perfect experience of the world in a way approximating divine experience. The nature of the full content of the spiritual perfection attained in saints' experience of the world can best be approached negatively by asking for the conditions under which it might be missing.

How could the intensity of the experience of the cosmological dimension of the world be minimized in a contrast with an appreciation of the world's ontological dimension? Or how could the intensity of the ontological experience of the world as created be minimized in the contrast, so that the contrast between cosmological and ontological perspectives is merely abstract and formal?

The distinction between the cosmological and ontological perspectives results from simplifying experience according to two different principles. The cosmological perspective results from simplifying experience so as to enrich it with intensity of contrast. This makes experiencers themselves the most valuable cosmological entity they can be. The ontological perspective results from simplifying experience so as to grasp it as a whole without the bias of one's particular location in the relative determinations of the world. This can be done either by extending concrete symbols to have universal range, as artists, religious people, and most others do, or theoretical explanation. A cosmological theory is part of the work of attaining an ontological perspective, although it might never be generalized sufficiently as to raise questions about the ground of the cosmos studied.

The function of simplification, the forming of abstract perspectives, is to articulate the concrete data of experience in terms allowing for intense sharp contrasts, reducing the need to block out things of importance. A "contrast" is a patterned thing in which unlike things are made compatible without being reduced to merely internal components of some third thing. The function of simplification is the *moral* one of attaining value in experience. The attainment of a cosmological perspective is directly related to acting in the world relative to one's own existential position. The attainment of an ontological perspective is only indirectly related to that, since it minimizes the location of the individual experiencer. But since the ontological perspective gives a profound contrast with the cosmological, it does increase the value of experience. Therefore there is an overall cosmological concern to live in such a way as to allow the ontological perspective to enrich human life. Not only should individuals seek to live this way, but societies ought to organize so as to promote and enhance the ontological perspective. The reason why one engages in either symbolic or theoretical ontology is not merely to understand or to have the perspective, but to enrich experience with it. The proper form for the symbols and categories is that in which they contribute best to the enrichment of experience. Saints have the richest experience of all, and in this sense are the most valuable of all people.

The answer to the question how the content of the contrast between cosmological and ontological perspectives could be minimized is that their terms are abstracted from experience in isolation from each other. Given the difference in perspectives, it ought to be possible to make the terms of simplification in the ontological perspective directly correlative with terms of the cosmological perspective. In other words: the terms of the ontological perspective ought to be relevant to particular and relative existence. When they are not, the contrast between the perspectives must be blocked out or distorted so as to de-intensify the contents of one or both perspectives.

Non-saintly people, if they have both perspectives contrasted only formally, suppress most of the feeling from the ontological side and retain only the most dessicated of concepts; ontology in this sense is merely academic. Spiritual people, on the other hand, who have a merely formal contrast, eliminate the intensity of their individual life. The problem for spiritual culture is to construct the ontological perspective so that contact with individual existence is not lost. It tends to get lost for two kinds of reasons, one common, the other more profound.

The common reason for loss of contact is that terms for articulating an ontological perspective tend to be very traditional. Symbols are traditional, and so are theoretical concepts. Yet the basic texture of historically relative experience changes, and the ontological terms which once simplified it faithfully do so no longer. This is not to say that the same terms have to occur in the cosmological and ontological perspectives, but that it should be possible to make an easy and fruitful movement from one to the other so they harmonize in the experiential contrast.

The more profound reason for loss of contact is the difficulty of attaining freedom from the psychic demands of the world. From the cosmological perspective, the given world is absurd, obligations make us seem unjustified, and experience is filled with suffering and evil. From the ontological perspective the absurd world is really united as God's creation, good because he made it, and bearable because of his love. If the transcendence of the world is accomplished, the temptation is to suppress the experience of absurdity, guilt, and vicissitude, and to turn resignation, thankfulness, and serenity into mere "forms of life."

The means to intensity of contrast in content between the ontological and cosmological perspectives is a feeling, appreciation, and understanding of the fact that God's creation is constituted by the intensity of individual experience in the cosmological sense. The ontological perspective grasping the world as a whole should appreciate it as God's creation, a creation consisting in the particular determinations or experiential intensities created. It should understand how this is so, since understanding is necessary to articulate critical appreciation, and it should have this appreciation raised to a high intensity of feeling.

God's creation is to be seen in terms of the immediate creative presence in each thing. Each thing's experience of the absurdity, obligations, and vicissitudes of the world is its particular portion of fulfilling God's creation. In spiritual terms, the ontological perspective is the standpoint of the creator who transcends the system of determinate things but is immediately present to each one as creator, the Buddha in the dung stick. The content of this perspective is the feeling of the experience of each thing in the world. This content must be abstract for human beings to attain the perspective in every case but one: their own. A person can feel his or her own feelings as created by God.

So the proper content of the ontological perspective is a return to the relatively given world, to the obliging values, and to the immediate quality of experience in order to raise the feelings of these to highest possible intensity. Saints who in the content of experience transcend the world are the ones most intimately involved in it. They face the absurdities of life with courage and resolution, as well as with resignation; they undertake the moral task with their whole energy and commitment of resources, as well as with thankfulness; they suffer the vicissitudes of life with a constant will to wring happiness from it, as well as with serenity. Put another way: true resignation, thankfulness, and serenity entail involvement with the world, an involvement which is fated to fail and bound for tragedy, and which cannot be sustained as the environment changes; but one whose essential direction also transcends the world. Mankind is both as dust and little lower than the angels just because of this contrast in experience.

The ontological perspective is a dimension of experience which must be felt, and abstract arguments can only suggest terms with which to feel. If the contrast between the ontological and cosmological perspectives does not enrich experience, then spiritual perfection is a lie, and like all lies must detract from experiential intensity in some way. Probably it would detract by distracting feeling from the cosmological aspects of the world as it is. But, by the same token, if the saints' experience is a greater intensity than experience without the ontological perspective, that is proof that there is content in the ontological experience.

Nothing has been said about the causes of sainthood. Fron the previous discussion it is clear that there should be two kinds of causes, ontological and cosmological. On the ontological side people have saintly liberty because God creates them with it. Religions testify to the fact that resignation, thankfulness, and serenity cannot be attained by work but come as gifts of God. The capacity to integrate experience with proper resignation, thankfulness, and serenity is a function of one's subjective processes in which God is directly present. Those characteristics mark the presence of God in its most valuable way in the hearts of people.

On the cosmological side, saintly liberation is a matter of human character. One is resigned with respect to the particular absurdities in the world given one, thankful for the particular values close to one's own experience, and serene in the face of one's own vicissitudes. One's spiritual liberation transcends one's world. And, on the positive side, one's involvement is directed to one's own world. Furthermore, the feeling of spiritual perfection is at the heart of the constitution of one's own experience. It is a matter of the determination of one's own essential features; in one's spiritual liberation one is most oneself.

The saintly peak of spiritual perfection is itself something to be celebrated and, since it is the most intense kind of human experience, its celebration is twofold: God gets the thanks, and the saints get the credit. This is based on the fact that God is the creator ontologically and people are cosmologically free.

The *content* of the saints' experience of God returns the orientation of human experience to the world. One is spiritually free to the extent that one engages in the other dimensions of freedom. Spiritual liberation is like a shadow between the autonomy of personal freedom and the participation of social freedom discussed in Chapter 1. Spiritual freedom returns one from preoccupation with oneself to involvement as an agent with nature and society. After one has made the return, however, the other dimensions of human freedom have new meaning. Without spiritual liberation they are merely ways in which human beings can be free and can appreciate their own freedom. With spiritual freedom they are also ways in which people participate in God's freedom or in the Emptiness of the Buddha. God's free action is the creating of the world; and people's intensification of their experience in free action, in all the secular senses, is the fulfillment of that creation. Therefore, with spiritual liberation the other dimensions of freedom add to the value of human experience not only their values in determining people with respect to other determinate things, but also the value of determining them with respect to God's self-determination. The fulfillment or greatest value of the other dimensions of freedom is not only in making the individual or society free, but in making them partially divine. Since God's freedom is constituted by the world, the fulfillment of human freedom is perfectly secular. But because that freedom contains the contrast between the freedom of the individual or society in the cosmos and the freedom of God creating the whole cosmos, it is spiritual as well.

NOTE

1. (Ann Arbor: The University of Michigan Press, 1960), p. 3.

5

Human Autonomy and God

THE PREVIOUS THREE CHAPTERS have spelled out many dimensions of human life involved in spiritual perfection or development. Together they depict a kind of freedom and responsibility which transcends what we ordinarily mean by personal freedom and social freedom. Of course, the spiritual ideals are ideals; whether anyone can achieve them, and to what extent, is something of an empirical question. But the ideality of those goals of perfection is something which must reveal itself when those goals are understood. I take it that the previous chapters have made out a prima facie case that it would be good for people to develop the virtues of the soldier, sage, and saint, properly understood.

Whether the previous chapters can stand with their prima facie claims, however, depends in part on my being able to put to rest three kinds of objections arising from other areas of inquiry. The first, arising from social philosophy or philosophy of culture, claims that religion, especially belief in God, inhibits people from attaining or developing their freedom. Because the arguments of the previous chapters have drawn upon ideas from religious traditions, spiritual liberation may be a disguised form of opiate for the people. I shall argue directly that the views of neither Marx nor Nietzsche, if true, would entail that religion's contribution to traditions of spiritual perfection need to corrupt personal and social dimensions of freedom.

The second objection claims from a theoretical standpoint that any philosophy which conceives of God as other than a finite and strictly limited agent must conceive him to be so overwhelming as to predestine human activity; this would eliminate personal and social freedom as theoretical possibilities. Now, the concept of God has not been directly examined in this book, and is not the topic. But, surely, enough reference has been made to the absolute or ultimate side of things that it is incumbent upon the discussion to come to terms with this explicitly. The third objection, of course, is that God cannot properly be conceived so as to be involved in human spiritual development in the ways depicted here, or that if he is, then indeed he is too determinate to allow human freedom. Furthermore, it has been a consistent thesis throughout this book that the concept of God, construed abstractly enough, is just a Western way of referring to the same things as Confucian, Taoist, and particularly Buddhist theologies or atheologies refer to, again construed abstractly enough.

After discussing Marx and Nietzsche, I shall pose the problem of predestination in as sharp a fashion as possible. Then, because that problem depends upon the concept of God, I shall examine that concept directly. With that concept clarified I shall then return to show how personal autonomy and social freedom are compatible with the views expressed.

The latter discussions are different in kind from the others. They arise out of theoretical considerations and must be answered directly in those terms, with specific reference to philosophical discussions. Furthermore, they are topics on which I have written elsewhere, and the special difficulties which they raise arise out of those other discussions; it is necessary to refer to those other writings for further clarification. Finally, these problems may not be real problems for the reader; if the reader has felt the bite of the problem of God, only then will the issues seem interesting to pursue. All these considerations make it appropriate that some readers might want to skip directly to Chapter 6 which returns to flesh out the problem of spiritual development. The present chapter is a kind of reflective hiatus in the overall consideration of spiritual liberation.

Marx and Nietzsche

Marx's argument was that religion, with its belief in the afterlife, its interpretation of temporal existence as not the most important arena of life, and its generally conservative social orientation, distracts men from the possibilities of making concrete improvements in social life. The argument is not so much an attack on the truth of theological claims about God as one on the social effects of believing such claims in the context of religion.

It is surely to be admitted that religions have often been conservative forces, identified with economic and political elements of the social establishment. But the history of religions also shows such establishmentarian forces to have evoked opposition expressed in prophetic criticism, and this in the name of the true religion betrayed by the establishment. Sometimes the critical reaction has succeeded and become the establishment itself; sometimes it has been squelched. But the element of religious social criticism in opposition to the conservatism of the established religion seems as historically inevitable as the conservatism itself. It is a plausible hypothesis that the dynamics of power in the conflict between establishment and reformist religious groups is a function almost entirely of the social forces distinguishing secular establishment and reform politics, having little if anything to do with religion as a special social form.

Religions do tend in some respects to interpret temporal existence as not the most important aspect of life. It is impossible to generalize for all religions, of course, but that tendency is to be found in both Christianity and various forms of Buddhism; both have come under Marxist attack. Regardless of the stances of organized religions, the basic religious thesis is something like the following. Temporal life by itself can be lived without God or without participation in some form of spiritual fulfillment. Spiritual fulfillment consists in part in being taken up into the divine time, into the plane of existence (or non-existence) wherein the world is seen from the divine or absolutely real perspective. This might be either separate from the temporal existence, as represented in theories of immortality, or a way of living within time as depicted in the three previous chapters.

But this is not to say that in its own way temporal existence is not important. Quite to the contrary of the criticism, the view of temporal existence from the standpoint of the spiritual adoption of the divine perspective has usually been a matter of prophetic judgment and a source of teaching about how to live temporal existence. The religious call to renunciation has meant renouncing one's profits from the social establishment as often as it has meant a renunciation of a concern for temporal justice. Although some religions in some places may have induced people to neglect the hard work of justice, there are enough counter examples to make the criticism inapplicable to the essential religious needs of life.

The claim that religion justifies acquiescence in the miseries of the status quo by promising a better life in the hereafter is surely true of some religious practices. True, that kind of belief is not characteristic of sophisticated and theologically acute religions; it is a matter of popular mythology. The Marxist criticism is directed not against theology, however, but against the effects of religion on people, especially those people whose theology is of only the most popular sort. The criticism holds at this point.

As remarked in Chapter 1, it seems essential to religion that it interpret the meaning of a person's or society's whole existence at the crisis times in life. Religion has always done that, and people naturally turn to it then. Most crises are times of misery, and often they are tragic—someone loses. Birth, death, sickness, initiation, marriage, war, discovery, all mean an end to something as well as signify a beginning. Furthermore, no matter how great mankind's technological power is conceived to be, whether through machine or witchcraft, people are sustained and destroyed by environmental factors beyond their control. For these things religion provides comfort by contrasting human evanescence with the absolute meaningfulness of the divine.

The response to the Marxist criticism is that in historical fact the belief in the afterlife and the function of religion to comfort have not always detracted from moral fervor and indeed have often increased it. As often as religions have taught people to wait for a better life in the hereafter, they have taught them that entrance to the hereafter is a matter of temporal moral effort. Not that "winning your way to heaven" is good theology—but it is popular, and that is the locus of the problem. Of course, the afterlife doctrine is often powerful in social communities where there seems little hope of alleviating present miseries; in these situations the doctrine performs the social function of making life a little easier. But when there is possibility of change, the social function of the doctrine is harmful, and the defeatist connotations of the afterlife doctrine should be rejected. But the question is whether they can be rejected without rejecting the religious part of the doctrine, the claim that everything temporal finds a place in the absolute meaningfulness of the divine standpoint.

There seems to be no real obstacle. In fact, the popular possibilities for temporal improvement can be interpreted in the light of the divine justice or according to the utopia of the afterlife and can gain added motive. The recent symbol of moral social leadership in America, the Reverend Martin Luther King, Jr., derived his fervor from just such a background of eschatological comfort for temporal miseries.

In conclusion, the Marxist criticism of religion as a source of social conservatism has only partial historical truth; sometimes religion has been that, and sometimes not. There is nothing essential to religion as a social response to absolute existence which requires it. On the contrary, religion tends to have social bite just because it recognizes that the divine perspective calls all human perspectives to account.

The Nietzschean criticism, in contrast to the Marxist, is that religion softens the self-assertion of human creativity by fostering weak and defensive personality types rather than the strong and unbound. Nietzsche's criticism was not against religion as such, but against the religions stemming from Judaism. He claimed that those religions bind the human spirit rather than release it. What he would prefer is a component of the Dionysian spirit of limitlessness.

The need for the Dionysian element in religion is compatible with the great organized religions, however. The interpretation of the spiritual soldier in Chapter 2, for instance, demands it. Although Apollonian religious types may write most of the history books, history abundantly exhibits the presence of and need for the Dionysian type.

Nietzsche's point is a defense of creativity as much as of frenzy, however. Furthermore, among the things which get created is a better human nature itself. Although Nietzsche may have been too sanguine about the possibility of improving human life to the level of a superman, he cogently affirmed the need to try, ironically agreeing with John Wesley that true life means "going on to perfection in this life."

Religions' contrary pull to this, a Nietzschean could say, lies in their historically bound symbols. Religions look to the past for their symbols of hope for the future. What human creativity might lead them to could not have been imagined in the formative periods of the great religions. How will the symbol of the "blood of the lamb" mean anything to a community which for ten generations has lived in a space city rocketing to Proxima Centauri? If our civilization is passing from the age of literacy to the age of electronic technology, then the religions articulated in the former age must find themselves anew. Nietzsche's point was that the established religions will fight this renewal, and will attack it by undermining the creativity making spiritual progress possible.

The religious sense of transcendent initiative is on the side of change, however, if change is indeed the manifestation of creativity. Creativity pre-eminently is a characteristic of the divine in most religions, except perhaps Theravada Buddhism. There is no need to deny the unique historical place of religious founders in order to allow that their salvific function will be conceived differently in the future from the way it once was.

We need not fear that a prima facie acceptance of the experiential testimonies of religion is intrinsically inimical to freedom. It is that testimony upon which the interpretation of spiritual liberation is based.

PREDESTINATION: A PROBLEM

But we cannot take the spiritual traditions seriously in their claims to truth if the theoretical objections to the compatibility of God with freedom are not rebutted. Does God predestine the world so that human freedom and responsibility are illusions? This is expressed in three objections.

The first claims that people cannot choose freely if God determines everything which happens. Most thinkers who make this objection opt for freedom and reject God.[1] But some, such as Luther[2] and Edwards,[3] choose the alternative. The objection is not the same as the alleged conflict between freedom and determinism, although Edwards and others did believe in determinism. The objection is that if God determines everything, one way or another, then he is the author of choices, and people do not freely constitute themselves through choosing. Rather, their character is determined by God, and the choice is not their own, *even if it is not determined by cosmological antecedents.*

The second objection is that human creativity is impossible if God determines everything. All apparently finite acts of creativity would be mere expressions of divine creativity, since God would be the author, by the first objection, of all human acts. The advent of novel forms and values in the world could in no wise be laid to people, only to God. Imagination could not be said to be possessed by individuals, but only to be a medium of divine creation.

The third objection is that people are not responsible for what they do if God is the real author. Responsibility rests on free choice, and if God is the author of human choices, then the responsibility for them should be imputed to him. (Remember that "God" here can be given many meanings, even that of Buddhist Emptiness; the objections could be rephrased to say that an "empty" person with "no-mind" is not enough of an agent to be responsible, etc., a line of objections argued against Buddhists by Neo-Confucianists, for instance.)

These objections are related to each other, but they raise a host of issues. If the objections are logically cogent, the theoretical options are to reject God and opt for freedom, to reject freedom and opt for God, or to change the conceptions of one or both so as to make the objections inapplicable. There is too much experience on the side of both freedom and God to make the rejection of either a possibility. So our main work is to examine the objections themselves and the possibility of altering the conception of God.

The argument to be made is that the objections are not logically cogent when rendered in properly abstract form. Freedom is not incompatible with a doctrine of a transcendent creator as articulated by a dialectical conception of creation.

THE CONCEPTION OF GOD AS CREATOR

The problem of God is not a cosmological one, but an ontological one. That is, the concept of God is not problematic in understanding what things there are in the world, how they are related, and how they work; these things should be explained in terms of each other by a system of cosmological categories subject to the general empirical tests of experience. God *is* a problem on the level of abstract reflection about what it is to be determinate at all, what it is to be a thing, an event, a relation, a process as such. Metaphysics can be conceived to be the inquiry into what it is to be determinate, to be a definite harmony of definite things, and although all our ideas are suggested by generalizing notions from this world, the metaphysical theory is intended to be applicable to any possible world having determinate things in it. God is a *problem* for metaphysics, but a solution to the problem leads from metaphysics to ontology.

Metaphysics aims to offer a system of categories descriptive of what it is to be determinate. The problem of God arises in metaphysics when it is asked why there is any such thing as harmony, why there is such a thing as determinateness. It is one thing to discover *that* some things harmonize, another to discover *why* they do. Pieces can be shoved around to illustrate *that* this arrangement is harmonious and some others are not. But no amount of intuition or rearrangement can explain why it is that things fit together harmoniously. The answer to the problem, it can be argued, is that everything determinate is created by a common source, God. The very meaning of creation is to make something composed of parts which harmonize. That there is a *common* source is the explanation of the mutual reference which things have to each other so that they may be determinate with respect to each other. And, as source, God is the ground for there being factual unities of the determinate things. God is not an element describing determinate things, but something transcendent of the things to which reference is made in describing them. Since the metaphysical system of categories is determinate, God must be the creator of that too, and transcend it. The category of "creating" is created and determinate, and entails ontologically a transcendent creator. The problem of God arises in metaphysics and the answering hypothesis comes in ontology, the study of why there is any determinate being at all.

The hypothesis is that everything determinate is created by a creator who transcends the entire system of determinations.[4] Because God cannot be determinate in himself, he can be called Nothing or Emptiness, with an appropriate switch of metaphors.[5] If God did not transcend the entire system of determinations, but was one of them, then the determinate harmony of God and the rest would be inexplicable; but that harmony is just the thing to be explained by the hypothesis. The conception of God, then, is the conception of whatever God is as creator.

At base, the protection of human freedom from divine encroachment rests on the integrity of determinate things. A determinate thing is what its determinate character is. Insofar as it has indeterminate elements, such as those alleged by some to be involved in free agency, it literally is not determined in those respects. If a thing has the special determinate character of determining itself further in some respects, that is what it determinately is. Its integrity consists in its being its determinate self.

The very transcendence of the creator guarantees this integrity. God's function as creator is to create determinate things, to create them together with whatever other determinate things they require in order to be their determinate selves. As a metaphysical entity, one has the integrity of being what one is because God creates one as such. But on the metaphysical level, God is not a determinate thing contributing conditional features to one as one's food or friends do; God himself is not a determinate thing to be taken into account in one's specific character. The integrity of one's specific character is completely a matter of one's own essential features and the conditional ones derivative from connection with other determinate things.

Cosmology does not need to take God into account at all; cosmology is the investigation of the system of created things, and need make no reference to their creator. God is not a cosmological entity whose influence on the world must be referred to as parts of the secular natures of things. Because God is the transcendent creator, the specific characters of all determinate things are free from him.[6]

Of course, God may give himself a determinate character in creating, and this could be something with respect to which people might be determinate. And he does at least give himself the determinate character of being creator (Emptiness is *this world's* Emptiness, not that of some other); so it is a transcendental characteristic of all determinate things on the metaphysical level to be creatures. But this binds no one's specific character on the cosmological level in which freedom is exercised.

With regard to a causal series, a distinction must be recognized between the causation, a cosmological matter, and the transcendental metaphysical status of the series as created. An earlier event is a cause of a later event if it is taken up as a condition and manifested in the later event. The specific character of the cause is determinate in some respects regarding what the later event can do with it, and perhaps indeterminate in others. The later event is completely determinate in its manifestation of the earlier event. Both events are created with their determinate characteristics, created determinate with respect to each other only in the respects in which they are in fact determinate with respect to each other. The earlier event is created as occurring earlier than the later event, in some respects determinate and in some not, regarding the way in which it will be manifested at a later time by the other. The later event is created with its specific character, determinate with respect to the earlier event but indeterminate in some respects regarding its own future influence. This is an analysis of the relation between the creator and a causal series dealing with the series as a nexus of public facts. Circuitous and repetitious as this seems, it is necessary for a straight story.

More directly relevant to freedom, however, is an analysis of a causal series in terms of the private coming-to-be of each of its actual units. In a present moment of coming-to-be, there is a process harmonizing three kinds of features.[7] First are the past facts providing the initial raw data to be unified so as to make a new definite individual. Second are the ideals directing the process of unification, the lures for integration; these are derived from past facts, perhaps, but they function differently within the process. Third are spontaneous features arising uniquely in the occasion; they do not derive from the past and they do not refer to the future as ideals; they are, rather, the novelties of actual decision, combining or rejecting, evaluating high or pushing into triviality the past facts to be integrated. Without the spontaneous features there would be no process; things would remain as they were given at the initial stage. If there were only past facts and ideals, there would be no subjective decisive process of adopting the ideals as definitive of one's own development. Of course, some processes are so limited with respect to alternatives that their spontaneous elements are little more than the subjective sensuosity of moving to the inevitable integration. But experience shows many human occasions in which the act of adopting ideals and of bending one's activity to them is a dominant character of the process; if this is denied, then there is no problem with God's interfering with freedom since there would be no freedom in process, with or without God![8] A process of coming-to-be is the integration of past conditions according to ideals projecting a future (at least the finish of the momentary process) as adopted and decisively acted upon in the subjective present.

Regarding the private acts of coming-to-be, God creates the spontaneous features of the moment. He gives rise to the decisive acts of the subjective process. Viewed from the causal commitments of the past, those features do appear spontaneous; there is no reason for them. Viewed from within the private subjective process, God's contributions simply *are* the present decisive acts by which the process exists as something over and above its past conditions. God is closer to us than we are to ourselves.

Each of those past facts, moreover, can be analyzed into what once were present occasions. Each of them pulled together its own past into new definite facts, according to its own ideals, and in a process which was presently spontaneous.[9] So as God was creating in those spontaneous elements, he contributed to the past of any occasion as well as to its present spontaneity. In fact, there is no element in any past fact which itself was a spontaneous act in some more remote past or other. Taking the time of things cumulatively, God creates them all in all respects.

The most general cosmological principle of causation is that any element in an existent thing has as its reason either the decision of that existent thing itself or the decision of some other actual thing or things.[10] All causal definiteness is to be traced to the activities of existent creatures. The general ontological principle of causation is that the spontaneous features of things are caused not by prior cosmological conditions but by God acting immediately. Those spontaneous elements simply are the acts of existence of things themselves. They have cosmological effects, since their public results are themselves conditions for further process; but they have no cosmological causes. From the standpoint of cosmological causes, a future event is indeterminate with respect to alternate ways it can spontaneously be resolved.

From God's standpoint, the act which creates the features appearing spontaneously in temporally existing entities is eternal. The features are temporal, occurring in their dated present moments. But their creation as determinate with respect to each other is not temporal. In fact, to the extent that they are determinate with respect to each other (and decisive spontaneous features must be determinately relevant to the data which they harmonize), they must be together in some eternal sense, however different they are in time location. There is an eternal creation of a temporal world in which earlier events are partially indeterminate with respect to later events.

Because all determinate things are created, there are no determinate principles of creation ontologically prior to God's creating. God is not bound to create one way rather than another. Any principles characterizing creation in general, such as that any created thing must be a harmony of other created things, come to be in the creation itself. Whatever norms there are binding God in creation are ones which he gives himself in the act of creating. In this sense the divine creation is perfectly free.

Consequently, the only determinate character which God has is what he gives himself in creating. There are four, roughly distinguished, levels on which God can be said to have a created character, with respect to which people might become determinate.

On the *metaphysical* level, God has the character of being creator, an identity which he gives himself simply by creating. Also, he is the creator of a world with determinate things in it, and therefore he has the character of creating harmonies, and so forth. The transcendental characteristics of every determinate thing simply as determinate are features which each created thing has in virtue of its being determinately related to God as creator. However, those features are not conditional but transcendental; transcendental features are abstract characteristics of the features harmonized; the features harmonized are concrete in the sense that the reason for them is in the decisions of experiential events. Only cosmological features are concrete.

On the *cosmological* level, God has the character of creating a world described by a particular cosmological system. Since the character of the world is empirically given, however, God could have created a different kind of world, one with no time, for instance, or no continuity of order. Whereas God's metaphysical character in principle is supposed to be *a priori* valid for any determinate world, his cosmological character is related to the specific world which he in fact created. On the cosmological level, God is the ground of spontaneity and of the objective continuity which spontaneity harmonizes.

On the *historical* level, God has the character of being creator of this universe with its particular history. Regarding events on a scale of historical significance to human beings, God can be said to be acting in history, since he is the ground of spontaneity exhibited by historically significant people, events, institutions, and so forth. Like his cosmological character, God's historical character is to be determined by an empirical reading of history. It is on this level that issues of theodicy are to be raised, for instance. In any historical event, the historical significance consists principally in how decisive action copes with given conditions. Since God is the ground of spontaneous resolution of decision, how things are decided can be read as how God acts historically.

This sense in which God acts as the ground of spontaneity is different from the sense in which the same events are acts of self-constitution; God is the ground of spontaneity in a decision, but the deciding is the self-constituting of the temporal event or agent. In contrast to God's cosmological character, regarding which God is ground both of conditions and of presently spontaneous features, God's historical character stems from the *human* significance of what he does spontaneously in historically decisive moments. Charles Hartshorne's description of divine creation as merely the fact that at no time does God encounter conditions which had not already been subject to his prior influence, applies to God's creation as historically significant.[11] Although the act of creation is eternal, the character which God has as an historical agent is developed "only so far" at any given time; the character which God has at a given time is temporally dated by the dates of the things created at that time. God's historical character at a given time is indeterminate with respect to what he will do at later times in just the respects in which the created world is indeterminate regarding its future influence. God eternally has the character that in the fourteenth or thirteenth century B.C. he raised up Joseph in Egypt, perhaps vaguely aware then that in the twelfth century he would have to get the Hebrews out of the country, but probably without any idea that he would have to do so with Moses, using the burning bush and other wonders. By the tenth century God's character was determined in all those respects: David was on the throne of Israel, and only the complaints of Nathan, the prophet, determined God's character in the respect that he would have to chastise the Hebrews through Amos in the eighth century. (The example, of course, is based on the supposition of the empirical truth of the historical claims.) God eternally has the character that his historical character at any given time is relative to the history which has occurred up to then.

On the *personal* level, many people claim that the specific character of the world is the kind of product whose cause we would call personal. We say that a man is a person and a dog is not because of a peculiar relationship between continuity of intention and the range and sensitivity of free choice in what he does and makes. There may be a similar relationship in the historical character of God as it is seen developing through time. In this case there is not only the empirical matter of determining God's historical character, but the classificatory matter of determining whether it adds up to a personal kind of agent, or something analogous to that.

In none of these four levels on which God might be said to have a "created nature" is there reference to a strong incarnational theme. An incarnational claim would be to the effect that something in the created world with a specific determinate nature bears God's nature in some sense. Because everything contains God as its creator, in this weak sense God can be said to be everywhere incarnate. A stronger incarnational claim would be to the effect that some created thing or person is the special agency by which God gives himself a character general with respect to all creation. If this created thing is a person, then God can be said to be personal in that additional sense. The person not only would have to epitomize the historical or personal character which God gives himself in creating, he or she would have to be the determinate thing in creation *in* virtue of *which* God has that character.

On the metaphysical level, God is the creator of value. Every harmony is a value.[12] "Making elegant things" is a transcendental characteristic of God's act of creation; he is the value maker.

God as the indeterminate creator of valuable things cannot be said to be valuable or good in himself. On the other hand, in creating, God gives himself characters of varying levels of abstractness, and these characters are determinate. God's goodness is a function of what he creates himself to be in the act of creation. It would be an interesting speculative problem to study how valuable God is in virtue of the fact that he creates this world.

This section has presented a conception of God in abstract fashion, showing in general how he is related to the world such that the world has integrity. The conception is rather like many classic conceptions, and not so much like the conception of God in process philosophy or in the philosophy of William James. Both Whitehead and James thought that God had to be finite in certain respects, in order to make room for human freedom. Whitehead considered God a concrete cosmological entity among the other entities of the world, and James went so far as to consider God to be a finite agent struggling with the rest of us.[13] The problem now is to see whether the strong conception of God as creator is able to make room for freedom. We shall have to consider the objections raised above.

GOD THE CREATOR AND THE INTEGRITY OF HUMAN FREEDOM

The heart of the problem as traditionally raised lies in the compatibility of God with three dimensions of personal freedom (these are listed in Chapter 1): freedom of action, freedom of choice, and freedom of creativity. It might be said that if God is the creator of everything, people are not the causes of their own deeds, they do not make their own choices, and there is nothing of which people can be creators. But there is no special problem regarding external liberties, for instance: if God provides the external liberties, they are there for people to take advantage of, and human liberty is in no way impeded. There are indeed various dimensions of social freedom possibly impeded by God; the obvious example is the freedom to make one's own opportunities based on one's own appropriated culture. But the impediments to social freedom come from the impediments to action, choice, and creativity. Therefore, attention can be focused on those three.

The way out of the dilemma is to argue that God is the creator and is responsible for everything in one sense, that people are free agents and creative in another sense, and that these two senses are compatible and in fact complementary.

Some thinkers would claim that this thesis, even if proved, would not be sufficient to show the compatibility of God and human freedom. They would say that human freedom involves the claim that people are completely free agents and completely free creators in all possible senses, and that if some sense of freedom can be specified which people do not have, then this just shows an illegitimate limitation to human freedom. If God is said to be a responsible agent in a way in which people are not, then he indeed limits their freedom to be responsible agents in that way.

Human beings are determinate things, however, and their freedom can only be of a sort appropriate to the determinate character which they have or develop. People would not be people if they caused the way God creates. God is the maker of everything in the sense that he is the creator of the spontaneous features involved. People are agents in the sense that they are spontaneous in determining themselves and their effects. God himself is not spontaneous. People do not create spontaneous features in themselves or in others. Although the spontaneity obviously connects people and God, it does not confuse the senses in which they make things and are responsible for what they do. If this thesis can indeed be shown, it is no objection to say that people ought to have God's creative power, that they ought to be the creators of spontaneous effects; it is non-sense to think that a temporal agent such as a person can cause a spontaneous effect.

Consider God's creativity in relation to human action, choice, and creativity respectively, beginning with action. Under what conditions would people not have freedom of action? Under what conditions would they be unable to do in the real world what they intend?

They would have no freedom of action if what they intend or would be willing to do voluntarily were impossible; freedom of action supposes external liberties.[14] It is a contingent matter in each case to determine whether what people want is possible. That God creates the world sets the possibilities in general, but his creating never inhibits freedom of action in the sense in which that action would be possible if God were not there.

People would have no freedom of action if there were no way by which they could affect things outside themselves. But the ability of people to cause external things is a cosmological matter, and experience shows that they have the ability. That God creates everything does not mean that people cannot cause effects outside themselves.

People would have no freedom of action if their actions could not be voluntary, that is, based on intention. But there is no conflict between God's creating everything and people's intentional character, because he creates them to be intentional.

In fact, God's creativity can in a sense be said to be responsible for the fact that people do have freedom of action, because God creates a world with people as intentional beings who can cause effects outside themselves in a world of opportunity. In this sense, God makes people free; he does not inhibit their freedom of action.

It might be objected that God is the real author of human actions, and that people only appear to be the authors. But the sense in which people are authors of their actions is different from the sense in which God is. A careful distinction can be drawn further between the sense in which a mechanical cause causes an effect and the sense in which people as voluntary causes cause effects. The distinction marks a difference in the determinate characters of two kinds of causes, and God is the creator of both kinds; as long as human freedom is a distinctive kind of determinate character, God is the cause of it and it has its own integrity as being what it is. People are the authors of their actions in any sense in which they can be held responsible for them; they are voluntary agents as a matter of determinate fact.

It might be objected further that if God is the source of spontaneity in the world, and the world has as much spontaneity as it seems to on a libertarian theory of freedom, then people are in fact virtually powerless to control anything in the face of God's power spontaneously to alter their effects. Now, it is true that people's effects consist only in the proximate facts which they provide and which the subsequent effect-events must respond to through the mediation of general laws. If the effect-event has much spontaneity of its own, there is little the agent can do to control things. This is just the way the world is; experience shows us this limitation again and again! But it also shows cases in which people do control their effects. People are continuous agents, however, and sensitive to the world's response to their efforts; they can change their tactics to cope with spontaneity. The mark of well-educated people is that they live well with spontaneity in others.

Furthermore, we must be careful to understand the sense of authorship exercised by the world's spontaneity involved in the impediment of a person's freedom to act. In one sense, God is the creator of the spontaneous effects. But the impediments to a person's action consist in something in the effect-event, or between him and it, distorting the agent's intended facts so as to produce an effect which he or she did not intend. And that sense of authorship is to be attributed to the thing in the world which distorts his or her intention.

Now turn to freedom of choice.[15] People are free to choose in that they can resolve alternative future possibilities on the basis of their own free decision.

They would not be free to choose if there were no alternatives in the future. But if there are no alternatives, it is because other specific determinate agents have closed them off, not simply because God creates everything determinate.

People would not be free to choose if they themselves could not decide as to what to choose. But if they *are* free, it is because the antecedent conditions are indeterminate with respect to the way the agent can resolve them regarding the future alternatives. That God created everything determinate, including the antecedent conditions, is not a categorical objection to this; God makes some things indeterminate, others not.

People would not be free to choose if they themselves could not decide what to intend about the future alternatives. They would not be free if there were an antecedent motive completely determining what intention they adopt in the decisive moment. But the subjective adoption of the reason directing this action is spontaneous. That God creates spontaneous features ranking the competing motives makes freedom of decision possible. Of course, it might be false that people do spontaneously adopt norms; this is an empirical matter. But even this would not mean God *could* not have created such spontaneity. The mere fact that he creates does not determine what he creates.

People would not be free to choose if the acts of decision were not constitutions by the agents themselves of what their own intentional characters become. But their characters are determined through the processes of ranking internal norms, processes which are their very inmost beings as persons. The persons as decisive agents are the processes of decision. Part of them is spontaneous in the decisive moment; but this is what it means to be decisive. They are spontaneous. The spontaneity is they. God is the creator of it, but not the effect. The spontaneous effect is the persons. Were the persons *only* spontaneous, they would have no human character, no personality developed from the past, no world to address the spontaneous harmonies to, and so forth; the fact that the spontaneous features harmonize the elements giving the persons identity warrants their claim to the possession of the spontaneity created in them.

One is responsible for what one chooses because it is one's own decision to choose what one does. One's decision is one's own constitution as the person who chooses this rather than that. Although one may want to deny responsibility, or to evade the consequences of one's actions, the fact that one decides upon choosing as one does is the justification for one's being held responsible.

People are tempted to let one off from responsibility for one's choices if they are persuaded that the choices did not stem from one's own decisions. That is, if one makes choices which merely reflect extreme conditioning by one's environment, or if one is in such a position that one never learned the importance of deliberately deciding what one's motives will be, people say that in a sense one is not responsible for what one does. But then it is clear that one *ought* to choose on the basis of one's own decisions, and at a mature age ought not to let one's conditions determine one without deciding to adopt them. If one cannot be let off as a child short of the age of decision, or if one cannot be shown to be ill in such a way as to be incapable of adopting a motive with a reasonably clear understanding of what one is doing, then one *should* be held responsible.

The responsibility for a choice is hedged within the limits of the real potentialities in the moment of decision. A spontaneous feature is a new potentiality and, if it resolves the process of ranking norms, it is a new element of actuality. In creating the spontaneous features, God adds new potentiality to one. But this only increases one's range of responsibility. It does not narrow it. God makes freedom of choice possible, not impossible.

The only way in which God's creation of the spontaneous decisive features in one might be interpreted as forcing or binding one's will in a way *contrary to one's more basic intent* would be the following. It might be alleged that one's decision must itself be made for a reason antecedent to the decision itself; God's creation of the spontaneous decisive feature would ignore the antecedent reason. But a decision is the *adoption* of a reason, not action according to one. There *is* no decision, or reason for decision, until the decision is made with its spontaneous elements.

The only way in which God's creation could be interpreted as the authorship of the decision would be if the decision were his product. Now, in one sense it is. But God does not produce in time; he is not a determinate cause. God cannot be said to be the author of the spontaneous features in the same way an agent can be said to be the author of his actions and their effects, precisely because in time they are spontaneous. Because one's identity consists in one's own occasions of harmonizing the features given one, the spontaneous features created by God are taken up as parts of one's identity. Because these features are uniquely determinative of the way in which one harmonizes one's given features, we can say that God is closer to one than one is to oneself. This does not mean, however, that God ceases to be God, or that one ceases to be oneself.

As with freedom of action and freedom of choice, so with the freedom of creativity.[16] God is the source of the spontaneous features involved in imagination. But they make up the people's imagination, not God's. The people are creative in the way in which their own processes of experience generally integrate their imagination with analysis and criticism so as to maximize the preservation of the old values in a novel order which constitutes new values. Although God is the creator of everything determinate, the specific character of being creative, like that of choosing freely or of acting freely, is a matter of determinate relations between individuals and their world.

To lack the freedom of creativity would be to be bound generally to repeat oneself and one's culture, to miss opportunities because one cannot think of novel means to take advantage of them, to be unable to act except in ways society has taught, to decide for conventional reasons. That God creates the world is not a special cause of any of these conditions in which creativity might be lacking.

To sum up this stage of the argument: in one sense God is responsible for everything, in that he is the source of all spontaneous features. He can be praised or blamed according to how one judges the resulting world.

In another sense people are responsible for many of the same events, in the sense in which they freely determine them to happen. If one throws a rock at one's neighbor, God cannot be held responsbile as the thrower. One is the agent of the deed because one's determination of oneself determined the event to happen. If God were to be held responsible as the agent, then it would have to be the case that one did not throw the rock but was doing something else at the time. God can be held responsible, however, as the creator of the whole world in which that particular rock-throwing took place and therefore of that rock-throwing. Depending on how one assesses the world, one praises or blames God. God's act is the creation of the whole world, and the rock-throwing part of it cannot be taken out of the larger context. God could have made a world without the rock-throwing in it, but only at the cost of eliminating one or one's neighbor, or eliminating free agency, or eliminating some other cause, natural or intentional, which put one within a stone's throw of one's neighbor. One's assessment of God must weigh all these factors; but in no way can that assessment relieve any particular agents within the world of responsibility for doing what in particular they did.

Now, human freedom is something understood by cosmological analyses. Therefore the claim that one is free in one dimension but not in another is a matter of cosmological analysis and cannot conflict with the metaphysical claim that, whatever one is or does, God creates one as such. Every event must be given two kinds of causal analysis, "causal" being understood in a neutral sense. On the cosmological level, its determinate characters are accounted for publicly in terms of the past factual conditions, and internally in terms of its own subjective process of coming-to-be; this is an expression of the "cosmological principle." On the metaphysical level, every event is created by God, whatever cosmology may reveal God to have created.

The conclusion is that, metaphysically speaking, God created a world which experience and cosmology reveal contains free people. Metaphysically, God is the source of the determinations constituting human freedom. Cosmologically, it is the people who are free and responsible.

Turning finally to the general objections raised at the beginning to the compatibility of God with human freedom, we may deal with them briefly in turn. The first was that people are not free agents if God creates everything which happens. This objection is a paralogism equivocating on the notion of cause. Human agents' causation is a matter of a relation between two kinds of determinations, their own character and that of the effect-event. God's causation is not a relation but an immediate production; only the effect is determinate. A human (or other cosmological) agent causes by relating created determinations; the divine creator causes by making mutually determinate relations be. God can create a causal series, beginning, middle, and end, all together. Unless he did this, there would be no possible relations within the series for agents to effect.

The second objection was that human creativity is impossible if everything is created by God. Again there is a paralogism, this time regarding the notion of creation. Human creativity is a matter of living a life such that one's agency brings about novel orders of affairs, which reinterpret, maintain, and enhance achieved values better than they could be maintained according to old orders. This is a matter of relations between determinations in the agents and determinations in their products, considered generally. Divine creation is the immediate production of a world of mutually determinate beings, related spatially, temporally, and in various other ways. God's creation apparently produces creative people.

The third objection was that people and God cannot be responsible for the same events. Again, their responsibility is different. People are responsible because of their spontaneous adoption of certain moral characters for themselves. God is responsible as the creator of spontaneous features; people are responsible as causal agents. God is responsible as creator of the field in which the events are caused by causal agents, perhaps by human voluntary agents.

The basic principle for reconciling human freedom with divine creativity is the special integrity of the world of determinations created by a God who himself is not one of the determinations. That has been spelled out now in terms of the distinction between metaphysical and cosmological explanations, human agency and divine creating, human spontaneity and the divine source of it, human freedom as a determinate character consisting of determinate relations between people and their world, and divine creation consisting of the creating of the whole system of determinations. God may be blamed for creating a world with only a little freedom in it. But he may not be blamed for doing something which a person might *otherwise* be free to do. God cannot coerce people against their will.

NOTES

1. See, for instance, Brand Blanshard's *Reason and Belief* (New Haven: Yale University Press, 1975).

2. See his treatise on Christian liberty, "The Freedom of a Christian," trans. W. A. Lambert, rev. Harold J. Grimm, in *Three Treatises* (Philadelphia: Fortress, 1970).

3. See his *Freedom of the Will*, ed. Paul Ramsey, The Works of Jonathan Edwards 1 (New Haven: Yale University Press, 1957).

4. This is argued in detail in my *God the Creator* (Chicago: The University of Chicago Press, 1968), chaps. 1–4.

5. I have tried to make out this case in some detail in "A Metaphysical Argument for Wholly Empirical Theology," in *God Knowable and Unknowable*, ed. Robert J. Roth, s.j. (New York: Fordham University Press, 1973), pp. 215–40.

6. See my *God the Creator*, chap. 4.

7. This is spelled out in my *The Cosmology of Freedom* (New Haven: Yale University Press, 1974), chap. 4.

8. See ibid., chap. 6.

9. This is a summary reference to one of the main tenets of process philosophy. The precise interpretation which I place upon these points is found in ibid., chap. 2.

10. This is Whitehead's "ontological principle"; see his *Process and Reality* (New York: Macmillan, 1929), p. 36. The reasons I believe it is better named a "cosmological principle" are found in my "Whitehead on the One and the Many," *Southern Journal of Philosophy*, 7, No. 4 (Winter 1969–70), 387–93.

11. See his *The Divine Relativity* (New Haven: Yale University Press, 1948).

12. See my *Cosmology of Freedom*, chap. 3.

13. These issues are discussed by Lewis Ford in "The Viability of Whitehead's God for Christian Theology," and by me in "The Impossibility of Whitehead's God for Christian Theology," in *Proceedings of the American Catholic Philosophical Association*, 44 (1970), 141–51, 130–40, respectively.

14. This concept of freedom of action is explained in detail in *Cosmology of Freedom*, chap. 5.

15. Freedom of choice is discussed in ibid., chap. 6.

16. This discussion of creativity follows that in ibid., chap. 7.

Spiritual Perfection in
the Contemporary Age

ANY CONTEMPORARY PERSON ought to be generally skeptical of the models of soldier, sage, and saint. If they are to be useful guides, they should be able to withstand skeptical scrutiny. The justifications for initial skepticism are legion. First and foremost is the fakery so prevalent in the spiritual business. People are so hungry for spiritual food that they will swallow almost anything, and pay large sums to those who feed them. The more exotic the spiritual teaching, the more promising it seems to the spiritually bored and impoverished, and the less able they are to judge whether it is true coin. The answer to this, of course, is not to ban the exotic but to appropriate and judge it.

Spiritual fakery takes an especially devious twist in the case of those who practice skepticism because the skeptical attitude itself can be represented as a kind of spiritual path. Tough-minded doubtfulness is for many people a form of self-flattery by which they believe themselves to have obtained psychic integrity in a world out to deceive them. Besides the implicit paranoia and fixation on feelings of adolescent rebellion in this attitude, it is a depressing example of bondage to an illusory ego; healthy skepticism is an attitude determined by something doubtable in the particular objects of knowledge, whereas sick skepticism is the identity which people attribute to themselves in the attempt to be somebody.

Beyond fakery, a perennial problem in spiritual matters, there are special reasons for skepticism in the contemporary age. First, the appeal to ancient models rests upon an appreciation of the experience out of which they come, and the plain fact today is that *no* funded experience is much respected. The role of experience is so important here that it should be explored at length.

Edward Conze, in his fine book *Buddhist Thought in India*,[1] remarks that modern Western civilization and ancient Eastern civilizations have different experiences which are taken implicitly as final courts of appeal. The West has come to see the methods of the empirical sciences as providing the paradigm of experience in terms of which all experiential claims are to be measured. Scientific experience requires developed expertise on the part of the experimenter, but the experiments are supposed to be public, duplicable in the relatively short run, and sufficiently isolable from the imponderables of complex existence so that they can be genuinely controlled.

The ancient East took its paradigm from the experience of yogis, people who by long practice make themselves into people who can have experiences which others just cannot have. Where the West has aimed at judging more exactly, the East has aimed at coming to exist consciously at a richer level of reality. Instead of a training experience which is essentially complete at the end of graduate school, the training of yogis must continue over an entire lifetime. Instead of being able to point out the critical phenomenon to other trained observers, the yogis at best can discuss common attainments of experience. Whereas scientific experiments are isolated from the larger context for purposes of controlled studies and then reinserted into affairs to manipulate them, yogic experiences are wrought out in the midst of life's conundrums. Conze's point was that whereas scientific experience is authoritative for the modern West, it would have been thought superficial and untrustworthy in the ancient East. In the East only carefully developed funded experience with a mature and severely disciplined paideia would have authority even though that experience is available to only a few.

All spiritual experience of the sort on which the heroic models in this book rest is closer to the yogic than to the scientific type. Spiritual experience is inward, and most of the outward manifestations usually associated with it should not be trusted. People who dress, behave, and make their living as holy people are likely to be frauds; truly spiritual people look rather like the rest of us. Certain aspects of mental discipline are now being investigated by neuropsychologists, and it seems as if the claims of spiritual soldiers to unusual powers are more often being corroborated by unusual brain functions than shown to be fraudulent. But the scientific investigation of brain corollates is far from advanced and probably can be applied within the framework of present theories only to certain aspects of mental discipline, not to the cognitive content of sagacity or the special loves of the saint. For those whose spiritual progress is not far advanced, it seems to be logically necessary for them to appeal to the authority of others' private experiences if they are to take spiritual perfection seriously. Contemporary people know to be skeptical of the *claims* which other people make about their private experience; since Freud we know to be skeptical even of our own claims to unusual private experience!

But there is a difference between accepting the authority of other persons' private experience and accepting the authority of an entire tradition. John Dewey talked about the "funded experience of the race." There are no isolable critical experiments by which this funded experience could once and for all be assessed. But it may be supposed that, as funded, the experiential claims, no matter how privately based, have been lived with the complex texture of life, that they have been repeated and corroborated in countless ways by many people in diverse contexts, and that over the long run they have been proved to enrich experience more than to impoverish it. That is, claims based on funded experience may be supposed to have an adaptive advantage. Most people would agree, for instance, that the interests of mature love ought to be allowed to dictate much of the order of the other passions of life, even if they have not experienced such love themselves. That human beings have a dignity which may be evoked by persistent respect is known not by experiment but by funded wisdom. That some people become wise through experience and others persist in foolishness through the same events is funded wisdom. Anyone who does not accept such funded experience, insisting that everything be "proved" to him or her, is and will always remain a fool.

The authority of funded experience cannot be created out of whole cloth, however. Respect for the traditional experience must itself be one of the products of the cumulative funding process. If one's own experience is not quickened by a respect for a fund of experience not one's own, one cannot legitimately be told one *ought* to accept a tradition on faith in order not to be empty. That is an evil form of authoritarianism and dogmatism, however frequently it is employed by keepers of spiritual traditions. Its evil consists in the rejection of the living quality of experience in favor of quasi-intellectual acts of faith. Most people refuse the act of faith and turn away from the possible experience. Those who do not are even worse because they come to accept a dogmatic representation of the tradition instead of being part of the tradition's experience itself.

Contemporary Westerners by and large find themselves alienated from any tradition of funded experience. Of course, this is not entirely true, and there are great differences between various groups. But not many find spiritual experience in their bones, and those who do are often those who have been isolated from the great trends in Western civilization. Most people caught up in spiritual enthusiasm demand quick and sensational results, closer to the proofs of scientific experience than to the lifelong quest of spiritual seekers.

Besides the attractiveness of the scientific paradigm, there is another reason for the alienation from traditional experience: namely, the diversity of traditions. The practical world within which Western people interact includes people steeped in Indian and Chinese traditions, in primitive cultures, and in various combinations of these. Furthermore, for all the dogged adherence to the scientific paradigm, most Westerners are aware of some of its limitations. They seek to recover sensuosity, contact with their bodies, a respect for nature and for quietness, and many other things thought to be better emphasized in various non-Western traditions. But if Westerners have ventured away from their own home, they have not settled in anyone else's.

The situation now is that for Westerners, and for most Easterners as well for other reasons, no tradition of funded experience is accepted wholeheartedly and, until it is, profound experiential claims must be regarded with some skepticism. From an abstract point of view it is hardly deniable that the *human* tradition lies there yet to be taken up, with values still unmeasured. But the difference between recognizing the human tradition and taking it up as a living enrichment with its own authority is the difference between idea and life.

The only answer is to try it. The inner authority of growing up with a vital tradition is most likely impossible to us. Our trials with funded experience must therefore be more provisional than would be the case for thoroughly traditional folk. We would be false to our participation in our historic time not to qualify engagement of traditions of funded experience with the ambiguity of continuing skepticism. Only when the human tradition has proved itself in our own cumulative experience, when it has taken form so as to have its own authority, should skepticism be put aside, and that will be done automatically.

With regard to spiritual traditions, the development of authority in experience comes easier than with many other kinds of tradition. Just because the relevant experience is personal rather than social, each development is somewhat self-authenticating and lends impetus to the next development. Whether one begins with the perfection of discipline, of sagacity, or of desire, the crisis of shedding the ego comes early. When the ego is abandoned in any of those forms, the desire not to be one who is fooled is also abandoned, and experiential curiosity is directed to particular cases, not to a defense of oneself. Openness to spiritual experience becomes self-reinforcing.

One of the most striking features of the models of soldier, sage, and saint is their universality. In one guise or another they have appeared in every major tradition. This testifies abstractly to their validity as models. It also means that they can be approached through whatever traditional channel seems most available. But it is very likely that the fund of experience which can be appropriated for the civilization now in the making will be at first an amalgam of many ancient traditions, not just one raised to prominence. We must therefore ask how the models should be specifically modified in order to be contemporary.

THE SOLDIER

With regard to our discipline, the ancient model of the soldier requires a sense of heroism lacking in the modern age. Our literature and art express more sympathy with the anti-hero than with the hero. But this is an intimate part of a general rejection of the possibility of authentic discipline. Not that heroes would not be worthwhile if we could find them, but they are simply not to be found. Those whom we had previously thought were heroes were corrupt and neurotic; their very discipline was a self-deceiving repression of psychic forces which could not be confronted honestly. We have come to glorify the people who confront their psychic dread and confusion and reel unheroically from its blow to abandon their sense of meaning in the universe. Kafka's Joseph K. is taken to be a symbol of the human condition, not merely a stunted human being. About the most which can be expected of people today, by the literary class, is a kind of brute affirmation of life and responsibility in a universe which justifies neither; think of Camus' characters, for instance. Worst of all from the standpoint of heroism is that if anyone tries to transcend the life of pragmatic politics and quiet desperation in order to attain a more heroic stature, that very ambition is taken to be a mark of dishonesty.

This critical aesthetic vision expresses the breakdown of the modes and paideia of heroism in Western industrial society during the first part of this century. It does not mean that heroism in other modes is impossible with other kinds of paths. New forms of heroism simply avoid the self-deceptions and emotional constipations about which the anti-hero is honest. Whether such new forms are possible depends on discovering new paideia. There is no philosophic reason why we should identify with the anti-hero.

Paths of discipline must be catholic and flexible. There are many styles of experience which must be respected in contemporary society, and each of these achieves discipline in ways partially idiosyncratic. Any given individual's path of discipline is likely to be syncretistic. This is very dangerous, of course, because syncretism in discipline lends itself to the tendency never to face an absolute showdown. When a given trial of discipline becomes demanding, the temptation is to be "catholic" and to try some other path. But the crucial events in a path of discipline are indeed the showdowns. One may practice thinking of oneself as capable of autonomous decisions, but the discipline is not firm until a momentous situation is faced and grasped with confidence. One may practice grace and focus of movement with T'ai Chi Ch'uan, but it has not become part of one's integrity until it has been exercised under the pressure of confusion and egoistic temptation. One may practice the yoga of mind control and self-observation, but it is not integral until it has become an attitude of serene awareness in critical times. Everyone knows the difference between devotion in church and devotion in the arena. However syncretistic one's collection of disciplinary methods, they must be put to the test.

Would it not be better to adhere to rigid and unitraditional methods of discipline? After all, discipline is a lifelong venture, and shopping around is likely to do justice to no method at all. Some people may indeed find one method which brings them through their own trials and crises, but most of us have trials unique at least in form to our historic time. Whereas the substance of human trials may be universal, the forms for which discipline must prepare us do indeed differ. The temptation of singleminded paths is to attain apparent success by disengaging us from the historical crises of our own lives. Westerners who devote themselves wholeheartedly to Indian yoga, for instance, often survive the crises faced by the rest of us by withdrawing from them; but this leaves their discipline forever in the practice stage.

Contemporary spiritual discipline must also involve explicitly technological elements. In a sense discipline has always done this; posture and breathing exercises, the use of drugs, the undertaking of ritualized trials are ancient technologies. An acknowledgment of the scientific age, however, requires embracing psychological technologies for what they are worth. Surely psychotherapy can aid in providing contact and control over them. To avoid these technologies would only be to alienate the process of spiritual discipline from the world which it is supposed to transform. The limitation of this point is that the technologies themselves should never be allowed to set the goals of development. The technical ability to bring about a change implies nothing about the form which psychic integrity *ought* to take.

To a degree marking an extraordinary contrast with traditional disciplines, spiritual discipline for today must be non-authoritarian. Many traditional disciplines have offered spiritual freedom later in return for spiritual submission to authority now. Of course, discipline is taught by masters to novices; this is the only way full experience can be transferred to those with little experience. But a contemporary master cannot demand respect for his authority; for the disciples to submit to demanded respect requires them to have an incompetent self-image, and discipline is ruined at the outset. Rather, the master must offer his help, at most seducing the novice to participation in a joint cultivation of experience. The master can be appreciated as authoritative because of his competence, not because he would rule the life of the learner. The word "master" is applicable only in the sense that he is master of his own discipline; he is not master of the learner. A disciple imitates the master in order to attain his or her own discipline, not in order to be a disciple of the master.

Because the bond of traditional authority between master and disciple must be weakened in the contemporary age, it would be useful to strengthen the bonds of peer community so that a seeker can check out the integrity of his or her new experience in a critical community. Good communities are very hard to find, precisely because we are alienated from the traditional values underlying communities. Many people must seek discipline by themselves, working out their own careers with little help except from their friends. But the authority of experience which serves as a norm for spiritual progress must be wrought from a process of democratic criticism. Some people, of course, have no standing to criticize because they have no discipline. But who these people are, and where they are in relation to particular stages of discipline, are questions which can be answered from no other position than the social process itself. Only those who come through the fire of real crises and are recognized by their society in the long run to be heroes of spiritual discipline can be our masters. There appear to be few around!

THE SAGE

The development of the soldier's will goes hand in hand with the development of the sage's mind. Proper sagacity for the present age is even harder to identify than proper discipline. From the beginning knowledge has meant access to power, and the sage's knowledge confers tremendous spiritual power. But ignorance in wielding the instruments of power is very dangerous, and the instruments are more powerful today than ever before.

The saint with the massive power to command but ignorant of the technological implications of what he does is a clear and present danger. Sagely
St. Francis was a minor disaster, according to the story, calling together his
people in the cathedral to pray about the plague, thereby infecting the lot.
Compare this with the specter of the saint who ignorantly deals with the
chemical technology of mass behavior control.

This casts doubt on the entire possibility of a person's pursuing the path
of the spiritual sage in relative isolation from the world. Perhaps everyone
with any power should be sophisticated in all kinds of knowledge, or else
artificially cordoned off from potential victims. Perhaps the walls of con-
templative monasteries should keep the sages in as well as fools out.

There is a more basic ground for skepticism about sagacity in the modern age. The experience which validates and reinforces spiritual matters
requires the appropriating of the human tradition in vital ways. What if
Western civilization in the nineteenth and twentieth centuries has learned
to live without the commitments involved in cultural appropriation? To
have appropriated a culture, however syncretistically composed, is to have
what Philip Rieff and other sociologists call a "moral demand system." Perhaps we have gotten beyond that to a true secularism. "Culture" is possessed only in its barest instrumental forms. Rieff, in defending this historical interpretation, writes:

> The wisdom of the next social order, as I imagine it, would not reside in
> right doctrine, administered by the right men, who must be found, but
> rather in doctrines amounting to permission for each man to live an experi-
> mental life. Thus, once again, culture will give back what it has taken away.
> All governments will be just, as long as they secure that consoling pleni-
> tude of option in which modern satisfaction really consists. In this way the
> emergent culture could drive the value problem clean out of the social sys-
> tem and, limiting it to a form of philosophical entertainment in lieu of
> edifying preachment, could successfully conclude the exercise for which
> politics is the name.[2]

Rieff finds the heart of the emerging culture in psychoanalysis.

> Freud's was a severe and chill anti-doctrine, in which the awesome dichot-
> omy with which culture imposes itself upon men—that between an ulti-
> mately meaningful and a meaningless life—must also be abandoned. This,
> then, was Freud's prescription to mankind as the patient, so that by the
> power of the analytic attitude a limit be set to the sway of culture over
> mankind.
>
> With such an attitude, men could not change the dynamics of culture
> (which were unchangeable anyway), but they could change at least their
> own relationship to these dynamics. They could become more diplomatic
> in their transactions with the moral system: not rebels but negotiators. To
> maintain the analytic attitude, in the everyday conduct of life, becomes the
> most subtle of all efforts of the ego; it is tantamount to limiting the power
> of the super-ego and, therewith, of culture. The analytic attitude expresses

a trained capacity for entertaining tentative opinions about the inner dictates of conscience, reserving the right even to disobey the law insofar as
it originates outside the individual, in the name of a gospel of a freer impulse. Not that impulse alone is to be trusted. It is merely to be respected,
and a limit recognized of the ability of any culture to transform the aggressiveness of impulse, by an alchemy of commitment, into the authority of
law. Freud maintained a sober vision of man in the middle, a go-between,
aware of the fact that he had little strength of his own, forever mediating
between culture and instinct in an effort to gain some room for maneuver
between these hostile powers. Maturity, according to Freud, lay in the
trained capacity to keep the negotiations from breaking down.[3]

Perhaps if the analytic secular attitude could be practiced ahistorically
and unreflectively, it could be what it seems in Rieff's description. But once
subject to philosophical reflection it becomes a "culture" itself, one among
many alternatives for appropriation. That self-referential paradox leads to
endless rounds. The secularist is not committed to a culture, he says, because there are no real objective cultural values, save that of truthfulness
to that fact. But must there not be a commitment, at least a resolution, to
accept amythic life truthfully? The secularist would argue that this is not
a commitment, in the sense of adopting a moral demand system, but rather
a grudging acceptance of things as they are. In light of such an acceptance
the best people can do is to employ the analytic attitude and tools to make
greater room for the humble pleasures left to man, those of psychological
satisfaction through therapy. Nevertheless, it must be said, resignation to
a life in which culture is merely instrumental to present personal pleasures
is still a cultural way of existing.

This is shown most clearly in reference to Buddhism. Far from being a
new idea, psychoanalytic secularism is remarkably close to many Buddhist
conceptions. There is agreement (1) on the threat to freedom posed by
both instinct and cultural norm, (2) on the strategy of analytic detachment, (3) on the need to live a middle way satisfied with pleasures which
have no large meaning, and (4) on the technology of disclosing the unconscious in order to gain control. There is even similarity on the point
of dealing with the goal of discipline when the validity of the goal cannot
be an object of commitment: "A monk asked Daishu Ekai (Ta-chu Hui-
hai), one of the T'ang masters, when Zen was in its heyday: 'What is great
nirvāṇa?' The master answered, 'Not to commit oneself to the karma of
birth-and-death is great *nirvāṇa*.' 'What, then, is the karma of birth-and-
death?' 'To desire great *nirvāṇa* is the karma of birth-and-death.' "[4] The
point is, if this pure secularism of Buddhism is a culture, indeed a spiritual
one, then so is analytic secularism.

Of course, the secularist would argue that the old values and cultures
are only myths and, having been recognized as such, are now dead. Knowing this, modern people cannot help but be secular. One does not *choose* a
commitment to truthfulness—that is to impose the old language of com-
mitment-culture on a situation which allows of no choice. Recognizing the

truth, one accepts it or rejects it. But rejection of what one knows to be true—or adoption of what one knows to be false—is itself a sickness, not only unfree but self-destructively so. Rieff writes of Freud,

> in the circumstances of modernity, to be religious is, he thought, to be sick; it is an effort to find a cure where no one can possibly survive. For Freud, religious questions induce the very symptoms they seek to cure. "The moment a man questions the meaning and value of life," Freud wrote (in a letter to Marie Bonaparte), "he is sick, since objectively neither has any existence."[5]

The issue comes down to what values one might hold, and to how one might hold them (rejection is one way of holding values); both of these are matters of culture. The straightforward way of dealing with this complex issue is to respond to the values and culture directly, appreciating, criticizing, and justifying them. The approach typical of analytic secularity, and exemplified by Rieff, is not to deal with the values and culture directly but as instances of types interpreted in a dynamic system. Values and cultural expressions are not to be naïvely responded to but to be understood as tokens within a system of the sociology of culture, according to this position. Instead of apprehending and criticizing what the culture is worth—a straightforward and direct confrontation—the social science approach is to see how cultural elements and values function within a system.

Philosophy must ask of the social science approach whether it can, in principle, do justice to culture and values. Is the human meaning of a cultural "bit" only how it works? Or is part of the meaning of a thing its intrinsic worth, to which some kind of ethical or aesthetic intuition is responsive? Certainly the experience of our civilization answers the second question in the affirmative. It is one thing to listen in astonished appreciation to a Beethoven piano sonata—feeling its aesthetic value. It is quite another to understand how the hearing of a sonata functions to provide human satisfaction, depends on a context of meaning, and so forth. Both responses —the aesthetic and the scientific—may be true. But neither can be reduced to the other. In the same way, understanding cultures, values, and commitments from a social, scientific, or psychological point of view may be useful; but it is mendacious and unconscionably reductionistic if it is taken to be exhaustive of the phenomenon.

Contemporary Westerners may well be beyond those cultures which call for traditional moral demand systems. And they may be beyond traditional kinds of commitments. But they cannot be beyond responsiveness to the values in their situations, including those presented in cultures made available for appropriation in some way or another. From the philosophic point of view, the questions are: Which values are better? What cultures are worthwhile? How can cultural elements be turned into relevant resources? How ought a group to relate itself to such resources? Whether a culture other than the secular one is possible is an empirical question, which takes the form: Are there valuable resources there for addressing the world? And the question should be addressed retail, issue by issue, not wholesale through generalizations about "modern man." Some people may be beyond cultural appropriation in traditional ways, others not; some beyond on all respects, others in a few or none. People respond quite differently to the conditions of modernity.

To be a sage, one cannot help being sensitive to the implausibility of much of traditional wisdom. On the other hand, it is the special feature of sage knowledge that it engage its object in the most direct and vital fashion. Directness of knowledge is the sage's norm, whether it be about oneself, or the world, whether it transform one's openness or tie one to the "mind of God." In the current age, however, every one of those kinds of knowledge has a counterpart in theory. There are psychological and philosophical theories about the self; theories from natural science, social science, politics, and journalism about the world; epistemological theories of transcendental openness; and theological theories about mystical union. Insofar as each of these theories represents a legitimate inquiry, each is dangerous as a tempting substitute for direct experience. In their tempting forms they never come whole. Rather, there is a bit of theory here, a proposition snatched from there. The sage is in constant danger of mistaking the mediation of theory for direct experience mediated by theory. This problem is exaggerated far beyond its extent in prescientific days when a sage in a cave could remain relatively uncorrupted by the theories of the day.

The only remedy for mistaking the abstract for the concrete is sophisticated attention to the difference. Only by being aware of what theories loiter in our language and common sense, and of what the formal commitments and relevant evidence for them might be, can a sage protect the integrity of direct experience. Unlike Chuang-tzu's hermit, a contemporary sage must be in sophisticated touch with current knowledge. No one should know better than a sage what the grounds are for skepticism regarding the interpretation of experience.

THE SAINT

There is hardly a need to justify the model of the saint in contemporary society. The spiritual path of saintliness addresses that awareness of the fragility of consciousness and of the deceptive and alienating power of inner passions which has undermined confidence in the heroic vision of Western society. Straightening out the knots of basic desires is the concern which has made psychotherapy and pornography such big successes. Who does not want to be able to love so as to will one thing? Who would not give a great deal, perhaps even undertake some discipline, in order to coordinate his or her powers into a powerful focus? Even those who would reject any implication of affection for an infinite God would like to find a way to become an integral part of the movement of the world, at the same time being just themselves.

One element of the perfection of desires does stand out as needing special emphasis in a saintly model for the modern age. When traditional cultures exercised strong sway over people, there was a kind of centripedal force exerted on the elements of life. Of course, it is always very difficult to integrate these into coherent loves. But the courses of the various realms of life—educational trends, politics, the sciences, the texture of human relations, and countless other elements which must be integrated into a consistency of desire—were not always as centrifugal as they are now.

Contemporary saints, therefore, not only need to gather and transform their desires so as to love God with all their heart, mind, and soul, but they must also love the art of living. Because the historical position of each person is unique, there is no rule for this life; living it is an art. The art of living is the manner of existing so as to gather into one life the greatest richness of experience possible, the enjoyment of goods, the fulfillment of duty, and the exercise of creative powers to their utmost.

There is a continuous tradition from Plato through Whitehead down to Erich Fromm which identifies the art of living at the maximum with *reason*. Reason has abstract components of contemplation and linear inference. Some of its parts are claims and theories of factual knowledge. *But reason in its integrity is the process by which one guides life*. Will is its instrument; desires, its subject. Reason is not just the logos, the structure of things; nor is it just inference or association from one thing to the next. It is a learned art of living as well as possible.

Consideration of spiritual heroes indicates that reason as the art of living involves considerable attainment of spiritual discipline, sagacity, and saintliness. The art of living requires psychic integrity; it requires self-knowledge, understanding, truthfulness, and enlightenment; it requires the perfection of the heart and its loves. The art of living requires spiritual fulfillment as well as a host of other things.

Reason as the art of living is a fairly comprehensive philosophical concept. From the standpoint of the person practicing the art, this reason means freedom. Not only spiritual liberation but all the personal and social dimensions of freedom find their home and their coordination in the art of living. From the standpoint of the environment affected by a person's practice, reason as the art of living means right action. The natural and social environment, as well as the personal environment of one's future are artfully served, in faithfulness to their relevant ideals, by reason as the art of living. From the standpoint of the absolute existence of things, reason as the art of living is attunement. The art of living is to accord with and enhance the harmony of all the world.

Another way of expressing this point is that the art of living is the cumulative perfection of responsibility. The point is not merely to do what is right, but to do so in an appropriate, free, human way; that is, with responsibility. It is hard enough to learn how to be responsible in one's personal and social behavior. How much more difficult it is to become responsible in spiritual matters. But can one be responsible for one's will without discipline? Arbitrarily to stop short of perfect discipline requires that one begin giving excuses to pass off responsibility. Of course, one may never have perfect discipline, but the art of living fully demands that when one face a crisis imperfectly one should reject excuses and accept both guilt for failure and a commitment to "going on to perfection in this life." Similarly, one should not give excuses for limited enlightenment or for being caught in the tangles of passions. Full responsibility requires working through all these, and the life of such responsibility is artful living itself. From the standpoint of responsibility there is a kind of "moral obligation" to strive for spiritual perfection because arbitrarily to stop the struggle at some point casts responsibility onto something or someone else. This turns the art of living one's own life into a mechanical process in that respect. The art of living is not only to accord with and enhance the harmony of all the world; it is also to take responsibility for one's whole being in that world. The tasks of soldier, sage, and saint depict the contours of spiritual responsibility.

The art of living is something slowly attained, if at all. The *love* of the art of living, however, is different from its actual attainment, and is a special desire in its own right. The explicit love of the art of living is an orientation toward life as a whole. It does not suppose that one has attained the discipline of a soldier, the wisdom of a sage, or the purity of heart of a saint. But it does suppose that one loves those things, and others, as parts of the art of living. It also supposes that one has a sensed ideal of wholeness in life, an explicit ideal giving content to the integrating love possessed by a saint. What the saint *would* be, that is the object of love in a person *loving* reason as the art of living.

In other more traditional times saintliness might be approached merely under the guidance of the appropriate wisdom. Skilled masters, benevolent communities, divine grace might bring a person to the purifying love of God which coordinates the desires of the heart. In our own centrifugal time, however, it is more urgent than ever that the would-be saint practice a special love, the love of reason as the art of living. Without this the desired purity of heart is likely to be a cheap version of the real thing, an integration purchased at the price of neglecting crucial dimensions of life. Spiritual reductionism is as much a danger today to the would-be saint as scientific reductionism. Without developing a special love of reason as the art of living, a saint can hardly be faithful to the multifariousness of contemporary experience.

Of course, love of reason as the art of living is philosophy, $\phi\iota\lambda os-\sigma o\phi\iota a$. In its original meaning for the Greeks, philosophy was not an intellectual discipline or a body of knowledge but a way of life. A philosopher is someone whose life is dominated by a love of reason as the art of living. If philosophers today have abandoned that old ideal, the ideal is still worthy and should be revived again under that name or some other.

The revival of philosophy involves more than reinstating it as a way of life. Philosophy must also be reformed as a kind of social thinking which provides relevant wisdom for the world. Academic philosophy has been derelict in providing the synoptic vision which society needs and which someone should supply. Only people whose sense of wholeness comes from a love of the art of living can make much progress toward such a vision. Philosophy should also be revived as a passion for contemplation, for understanding things in whatever terms are most appropriate, for the sheer joy of understanding; of all the meanings of original philosophy, this one has survived best down to the present day, even though it has suffered from the proliferation of philosophical specialties. Of most concern for spiritual liberation, however, is the revival of philosophy as a way of life, a life dominated by the love of reason as the art of living.

Philosophy is not saintliness. A philosopher loves a wholeness which includes what the saint possesses. A philosopher need have only limited spiritual attainments in discipline, divine sagacity, and saintliness in order to be faithful to his or her love, so long as full responsibility is firmly pursued. But the pursuit of that love must lead down spiritual paths among others. Both the philosopher and the saint are characterized by their loves. A philosopher loves the art of living and a saint loves God and absolute existence of the world as God creates it. To have philosophic love is to be oriented in the philosophical life, but perhaps not to have attained much. The saint's love itself is the greatest of spiritual attainments.

For a philosopher, spiritual perfection is only one of many elements to be incorporated into the tasks of the art of living. As one among several it competes with the others for time and energy, and receives attention according to the art which shapes the contours of the particular philosopher's life. Spiritual matters weigh heavily for some philosophers, lightly for others. Philosophers may be artistic, political, sporting, craftsmanly, academic, mainly intellectual, or a whole variety of other emphases which may compete with spiritual liberation as long as the demand of perfect responsibility is addressed.

A saint, however, must be more philosophical in this age than in most others. With the fragmentation of all life, the love of reason as the art of living is a necessary guide to the wholeness of heart which consists in the love of God and his creation. Not to be philosophical in this sense is for the would-be saint to run inordinate risks not only of partiality but of the diverse reductionisms of experience which seem to be the price required for sanity. An unphilosophical saint is likely to have attained purity of heart by denying the very engagements with experience which make life human today.

Some people argue, on the basis of historical example, that saints can be non-historical, essentially disengaged from the affairs of their day, otherworldly. To focus on the knowledge and love of God is to orient oneself away from history, and if the love of God turns one back to service in the world, duties are obvious enough not to require being of the world.

But the conception of saintliness described above does not allow this. Saints do not deny participation in the world in favor of participation in the divine; that model is rightly rejected in twentieth-century criticisms of the heroic mold. Saints, rather, coordinate the desires by which they participate in the world so that they harmonize in a grand love of God and the world as God's creation, or harmonize in a grand embrace of No-mind. The demand for harmony sets limits to the extent of any of the saints' worldly passions. But the harmony is not based on a principle of self-contained ego identity. The harmony is based on being faithful to the enhancement of the world according to its diverse ideals; saints love in harmony with the universe, as God does in creating. As God is immediately present in any finite thing, so saints at least aim to participate in the inmost being of each thing. The saints participate in the world more, not less, than do those who identify themselves with a particular mode of endeavor. Because saints are equally close to all things, the only reasons for their actions are the objective merits of the alternatives faced. The saints' limitations in participation are set only by the energy which must be spent in the perfection of their own hearts. A worthy political cause, for instance, may in the short run profit more from an egoistic person bent on identifying with justice than on a saint who may not have time for the mimeograph machine. That saints are a perfection of humanity does not always mean that they do the most good.

There is no reason why fully sensitive and engaged participants in the affairs of our day cannot adopt as models for their own spiritual development those of the soldier, the sage, and the saint. The models are instructive regarding where they are and how far they have to go. They provide orientation points for understanding the many dimensions of the struggle. They even render it possible for twentieth-century pilgrims to see themselves as making the same journey as countless others in ages long past and cultures astonishingly diverse. Spiritual perfection—the attainment of psychic integrity through the discipline of a soldier, the wisdom of a sage, and saintly perfection of the heart—is one of the most profound endeavors of mankind.

SUCCESS AND FAILURE

What is the measure of success here? The logic of taking models as guides to life is complex. The model can be described as if it were embodied in real persons. But there is a difference between the ideal modes as described here and any persons who might embody them. The embodiment is always too particular, too historical, too idiosyncratic. Furthermore, there exist hardly any concrete embodiments of the models, unless we lower our standards for actual fact. The soldier, the sage, and the saint are muses who define the contours of life when adopted as ideal models.

For many of us spiritual development is at best an affair of ambiguous success and distressing failures. If we enter the spiritual path we wobble from one model to another as the occasion demands; progress in the pursuit of each requires success in the other, yet our efforts are uneven. If we had to guarantee the possibility of transcendent accomplishment before starting we would never begin.

Spiritual perfection is an essential ideal for human life, however. Completely to ignore it is to shut off any responsiveness to the demands of existence on our integrity. Most of us therefore give spiritual development some attention from time to time, even if we tell ourselves that enough is enough. And if we are very attentive, the failures and backslidings may seem more vivid than any advance in psychic integrity.

Like any life lived in pursuit of an ideal essential to human existence—the political life, the artistic life, the life of connoisseurship, the productive life, the philosophic life—the life of the spiritual seeker is potentially tragic. The ideal can catch one up until one has pretentions which fate inevitably will strike down. No statesman's justice and peace can be as good as it should be; no soldier's discipline, sage's wisdom, or saint's virtue can perfect the human spirit. Because true engagement with the normative side of life means identifying more with one's ideals than with one's actual accomplishments, the poignancy of failure cuts to the heart of one's self.

There is a special advantage to the spiritual path. From the very beginning, the path of spiritual liberation initiates the destruction of the self. To the extent this process succeeds even a bit, the tragedy becomes only external. The true spiritual seekers fail only in the eye of the observer. As for themselves, they are not failures and not tragic because they themselves are nothing substantial which might fail.

All the spiritual traditions agree that the path of spiritual liberation is paradoxical. On the one hand it is the infinitely difficult task of human perfection. On the other, to be engaged in the task is proof itself that liberation has not been attained. The answer to the spiritual quest is that there is no spiritual attainment. Nirvāṇa is Saṁsāra. The kingdom of heaven is already at hand and the world has been overcome. Of course, the realization of this requires a life of extraordinary discipline, sagacity, and purity of heart. Prometheus in his discipline, Apollo in his wisdom, and Eros in his love find their mirror in Dionysius. Yet Dionysius would not be divine were it not for the others. The Zen master said, "Not to commit oneself to the karma of birth-and-death is great *nirvāṇa*. . . . To desire great *nirvāṇa* is the karma of birth-and-death." How great must be the love of one whose soul is so entire as not to feel the need for liberation!

NOTES

1. (Ann Arbor: The University of Michigan Press, 1967), pp. 17ff.
2. *The Triumph of the Therapeutic* (New York: Harper & Row, 1966), p. 26.
3. Ibid., pp. 30–31.
4. Daisetz T. Suzuki, *Zen and Japanese Culture*, Bollingen Series LXIV (Princeton: Princeton University Press, 1959), p. 139.
5. *Triumph of the Therapeutic*, pp. 33–34.

Bibliography

Ahlstrom, Sydney E. *A Religious History of the American People*. New Haven: Yale University Press, 1972.

Barraclough, Geoffrey. *An Introduction to Contemporary History*. Baltimore: Penguin, 1967.

Bellah, Robert N. *The Broken Covenant: American Civil Religion in Time of Trial*. New York: Seabury, 1975.

Berger, Peter L. *The Sacred Canopy*. Garden City, N.Y.: Doubleday Anchor, 1969.

Blanshard, Brand. *Reason and Belief*. New Haven: Yale University Press, 1975.

Bultmann, Rudolf. *Theology of the New Testament*. Trans. Kendrick Grobel. 2 vols. New York: Scribner, 1951.

Castaneda, Carlos. *Journey to Ixtlan*. New York: Simon & Schuster, 1972.

———. *A Separate Reality*. New York: Pocket, 1972.

———. *Tales of Power*. New York: Simon & Schuster, 1974.

———. *The Teachings of Don Juan*. New York: Ballantine, 1969.

Chan, Wing-tsit, ed. and trans. *A Sourcebook in Chinese Philosophy*. Princeton: Princeton University Press, 1963.

Chang, Garma C. C. *The Buddhist Teaching of Totality*. University Park: Pennsylvania State University Press, 1971.

Conze, Edward. *Buddhist Thought in India*. Ann Arbor: The University of Michigan Press, 1967.

Creel, Herrlee G. *What Is Taoism?* Chicago: The University of Chicago Press, 1970.

Delza, Sophia. *T'ai Chi Ch'uan*. New York: McKay, 1961.

Dewey, John. *Theory of Valuation*. International Encyclopedia of Unified Science, vol. 2, part 4. Chicago: The University of Chicago Press, 1939.

Edwards, Jonathan. *Freedom of the Will*. Ed. Paul Ramsey. The Works of Jonathan Edwards I. New Haven: Yale University Press, 1957.

———. *The Nature of True Virtue*. Ed. William K. Frankena. Ann Arbor: The University of Michigan Press, 1960.

———. *The Religious Affections*. Ed. John E. Smith. The Works of Jonathan Edwards II. New Haven: Yale University Press, 1959.

Eliade, Mircea. *The Sacred and the Profane*. Trans. Willard R. Trask. New York: Harper Torchbooks, 1961.

———. *Shamanism: Archaic Techniques of Ecstasy*. Trans. Willard R. Trask. Bollingen Series LXXVI. Princeton: Princeton University Press, 1964.

———. *Yoga: Immortality and Freedom*. Trans. Willard R. Trask. Bollingen Series LVI. Princeton: Princeton University Press, 1958.

Fingarette, Herbert. *Confucius: The Secular as Sacred*. New York: Harper Torchbooks, 1972.

———. *The Self in Transformation: Psychoanalysis, Philosophy, and the Life of the Spirit*. New York: Basic, 1963.

Ford, Lewis. "The Viability of Whitehead's God for Christian Theology."

    Proceedings of the American Catholic Philosophical Association, 44 (1970), 141–51.

Freud, Sigmund. *The Future of an Illusion*. Trans. W. D. Robson-Scott. Ed. James Strachey. Garden City, N.Y.: Doubleday Anchor, 1964.

——. *A General Selection from the Works of Sigmund Freud*. Ed. John Rickman. Garden City, N.Y.: Doubleday Anchor, 1957.

Golding, William. *Lord of the Flies*. New York: Capricorn, 1959.

Hartshorne, Charles. *The Divine Relativity*. New Haven: Yale University Press, 1948.

Havelock, Eric A. *Preface to Plato*. Cambridge: Harvard University Press, 1963.

Heidegger, Martin. *Existence and Being*. Trans. Werner Brock. Chicago: Regnery, 1949.

Hinton, William. *Fanshen*. New York: Vintage, 1966.

Huang Po. *The Zen Teaching of Huang Po on the Transmission of Mind*. Trans. John Blofeld. New York: Grove, 1958.

Hui-neng. *The Platform Sutra of the Sixth Patriarch*. Trans. Philip B. Yampolsky. New York: Columbia University Press, 1967.

Humphreys, Christmas, ed. *The Wisdom of Buddhism*. New York: Harper Colophon, 1970.

Jaspers, Karl. *Reason and Existenz*. Trans. William Earle. New York: Noonday, 1957.

Luther, Martin. "The Freedom of a Christian." Trans. W. A. Lambert. Rev. Harold J. Grimm. *Three Treatises*. Philadelphia: Fortress, 1970.

McNeill, William. *The Rise of the West*. Chicago: The University of Chicago Press, 1963.

Marx, Karl, and Engels, Friedrich. *Basic Writings on Politics and Philosophy*. Ed. Lewis S. Feuer. Garden City, N.Y.: Doubleday Anchor, 1959.

May, Rollo. *Love and Will*. New York: Norton, 1969.

Needleman, Jacob. *The New Religions*. Garden City, N.Y.: Doubleday, 1970.

Neville, Robert C. *The Cosmology of Freedom*. New Haven: Yale University Press, 1974.

——. *God the Creator*. Chicago: The University of Chicago Press, 1968.

——. "The Impossibility of Whitehead's God for Christian Theology." *Proceedings of the American Catholic Philosophical Association*, 44 (1970), 130–40.

——. "Whitehead on the One and the Many." *Southern Journal of Philosophy*, 7, No. 4 (Winter 1969–70), 387–93.

Nietzsche, Friedrich. *The Birth of Tragedy* and *The Genealogy of Morals*. Trans. Francis Golffing. Garden City, N.Y.: Doubleday Anchor, 1956.

——. *Thus Spoke Zarathustra*. Trans. Marianne Cowan. Chicago: Regnery, 1957.

Nitobe, Inazo. *Bushido: The Soul of Japan*. Rutland, Vt.: Tuttle, 1969.

Plato. *Dialogues*. Edd. Edith Hamilton and Huntington Cairns. Bollingen Series LXXI. Princeton: Princeton University Press, 1961.

Radhakrishnan, Sarvepalli, and Moore, Charles A., eds. *A Sourcebook in Indian Philosophy*. Princeton: Princeton University Press, 1957.

Ricoeur, Paul. *The Symbolism of Evil*. Trans. Emerson Buchanan. Boston: Beacon, 1969.

Rieff, Philip. *The Triumph of the Therapeutic*. New York: Harper & Row, 1966.

Roth, Robert J., S.J. *God Knowable and Unknowable*. New York: Fordham University Press, 1973.

Smith, John E. *Experience and God.* New York: Oxford University Press, 1968.
——. *Reason and God.* New Haven: Yale University Press, 1961.
Suzuki, Daisetz T. *Zen and Japanese Culture.* Bollingen Series LXIV. Princeton: Princeton University Press, 1959.
Tillich, Paul. *Christianity and the Encounter of the World Religions.* New York: Columbia University Press, 1963.
——. *Theology of Culture.* Ed. Robert C. Kimball. New York: Oxford University Press, 1959.
Weiss, Paul. *The God We Seek.* Carbondale: Southern Illinois University Press, 1964.
Wesley, John. *A Compend of Wesley's Theology.* Edd. Robert W. Burtner and E. Chiles. Nashville: Abingdon, 1954.
Whitehead, Alfred North. *Process and Reality.* New York: Macmillan, 1929.
——. *Religion in the Making.* New York: Macmillan, 1926.

Index

Absolute, 10–13, 43–45, 78, 82, 87

Absolute values, Standpoint concerning, 81–83

Achilles, 3

Action, 10, 12, 29–38, 44, 52, 55–61, 72, 75; as political or religious, 15–17; defined in Bhagavad-gita, 35; Freedom of, 8; prior to reason and appetite, 36; Yoga of, 35–38

Adoption, 101

Aesthetics, 44, 54, 121, 125, 131

Alienation, 11, 17, 23, 42

America, 15, 17, 23

Anger, 6

Anselm, St., 66

Antinomianism, 40

Appetite, 6, 36, 45

Archetype, 7

Aristotle, 28

Arjuna, 1, 35–37

Art of living, 127–30

Assertion of self (self-will), 29–33

Atheism, 12, 43–44, 65

Athletics, 33–35, 43

Attachment, 10, 35, 87

Attunement, 48, 127

Authority, 7, 16, 18, 118–20

Authorship, Double-agent theory of, 67–69

Autonomy, 8, 11, 17, 100

Beauty, 11

Becoming, 6, 72

Being, 7, 44, 72, 91

Bellah, Robert, 17

Belonging, Sense of, 13–15

Benevolence, to being in general, 82, 90–91

Berger, Peter, 12

Bhagavad-gita, 35–37, 43

Bible, The, 15

Body, 34, 47, 84, 119

Bondage, 8, 30, 39, 41

Brahman, 64

Brahmanism, 2

Buddha, 3–4, 46, 48, 63, 95, 97

Buddhism, 1, 2, 10, 12, 16, 20, 27, 41–43, 63–64, 66, 79, 99, 100–101, 124; Northern and Southern Ch'an, 41–42; Mahāyāna, 16, 68; Theravada, 103; Zen, 1, 35, 68, 131

Camus, Albert, 120

Capitalism, 16

Castaneda, Carlos, 20

Causal definiteness, 106–10

Cause, 6, 21, 44, 64, 67–69, 80, 92–98, 105, 110–15; Cosmological vs. ontological, 62–63, 65–66; Deterministic, 31, 103–15

Character, 33, 43, 45, 49, 51, 82–83; defined by approved desires, 32; of God, 65–66, 85; Ontological vs. cosmological, 64–66; Reformation of, 58–62

China, 12, 16, 18, 21–22, 65, 119

Chivalry, 23

Choice, 1, 12, 14–15, 23, 77–79, 88; Freedom of, 8

Chosen People, 13

Christianity, 1, 2, 14, 16, 21, 66, 88, 100–101; Protestant, 16–17

Chuang-tzu, 2, 126

Classes (Methodist cell groups), 17

Cognition, 27, 39, 44, 52

Communication, 14–15

Community, 15–18; as check on spiritual authenticity, 122

Complexity, 81

Conatus, 28

Concentration, 44–45

Concept, 5, 59, 66; used for feeling, 54–56

Confidence in self, 29–33

Confucianism, 18, 27, 66, 99; Han, 16

Confucius, 2, 3, 46

Connoisseurship, 41, 81

Consciousness, 29, 39–43, 45, 47, 49, 118, 126

Contingency, 64–67

Contrast, 62, 93–97

Conversion, 17, 23

Conze, Edward, 117

Cosmological perspective, 87

Cosmology, 9–12, 40–41, 43–44, 64, 78, 82, 94, 104–105; as religious function, 12–15; defined, 24n; Displacement from religion to philosophy and science, 18–19; Ground of world, 65–66, 91–98

Courage, 3–4, 55

137